T0212480

Lecture Notes
in Business Information Processing   **285**

More information about this series at http://www.springer.com/series/7911

Felix Piazolo · Verena Geist
Lars Brehm · Rainer Schmidt (Eds.)

Innovations in Enterprise Information Systems Management and Engineering

5th International Conference, ERP Future 2016 - Research
Hagenberg, Austria, November 14, 2016
Revised Papers

 Springer

Editors
Felix Piazolo
Andrassy University Budapest
Budapest
Hungary

Verena Geist
Software Competence Center Hagenberg
Hagenberg
Austria

Lars Brehm
Munich University of Applied Sciences
Munich
Germany

Rainer Schmidt
Munich University of Applied Sciences
Munich
Germany

ISSN 1865-1348   ISSN 1865-1356   (electronic)
Lecture Notes in Business Information Processing
ISBN 978-3-319-58800-1   ISBN 978-3-319-58801-8   (eBook)
DOI 10.1007/978-3-319-58801-8

Library of Congress Control Number: 2017940245

Printed on acid-free paper

This Springer imprint is published by Springer Nature
The registered company is Springer International Publishing AG
The registered company address is: Gewerbestrasse 11, 6330 Cham, Switzerland

Preface

This book contains revised papers from the ERP Future 2016—Research Conference, held in Hagenberg, Austria, in November 2016. The 12 papers presented in this volume were carefully, peer-reviewed and selected from a total of 29 submissions.

The ERP Future—Research Conference is a platform for research in ERP systems and closely related topics such as business processes, business intelligence, and enterprise information systems. The submitted contributions cover these topics from a business and a technological point of view, with high theoretical as well as practical impact.

February 2017

Felix Piazolo
Verena Geist
Lars Brehm
Rainer Schmidt

Organization

Program Committee

Martin Adam	University of Applied Sciences Kufstein, Austria
Rogerio Atem de Carvalho	Instituto Federal Fluminense, Brazil
Dagmar Auer	Johannes Kepler University Linz, Austria
Irene Barba Rodriguez	University of Seville, Spain
Josef Bernhart	EURAC Bozen/Bolzano, Italy
Miklos Biro	Software Competence Center Hagenberg, Austria
Goetz Botterweck	Lero - The Irish Software Engineering Research Centre, Ireland
Ruth Breu	University of Innsbruck, Austria
Oliver Christ	ZHAW Zurich University of Applied Sciences, Switzerland
Jörg Courant	HTW Berlin, Germany
Maya Daneva	University of Twente, The Netherlands
Dirk Draheim	University of Innsbruck, Austria
Jörg Dörr	Fraunhofer IESE, Germany
Sandy Eggert	Berlin School of Economics and Law, Germany
Kerstin Fink	University of Innsbruck, Austria
Kai Fischbach	University of Bamberg, Germany
Johann Gamper	Free University of Bozen-Bolzano, Italy
Norbert Gronau	University of Potsdam, Germany
Hans H. Hinterhuber	University of Innsbruck, Austria
Sami Jantunen	Lappeenranta University of Technology, Finland
Asmamaw Mengistie	Sholla Computing, USA
David Meyer	University of Applied Sciences Technikum Wien, Austria
Christine Natschläger	Software Competence Center Hagenberg, Austria
Wolfgang Ortner	Joanneum University of Applied Sciences, Austria
Lukas Paa	Andrassy University Budapest, Hungary
Kurt Promberger	University of Innsbruck, Austria
Friedrich Roithmayr	Johannes Kepler University Linz, Austria
Tomislav Rozman	DOBA Faculty of Applied Business and Social Studies, Slovenia
Matthias Schumann	University of Göttingen, Germany
Stéphane S. Somé	University of Ottawa, Canada
Alfred Taudes	WU—Vienna University of Economics and Business, Austria
Victoria Torres Bosch	Polytechnic University of Valencia, Spain

Contents

Introduction of Enterprise Systems

Key Factors for Successful ERP Implementation: Case Studies from Private and Public Organizations in Thailand

Paweena Wanchai[(✉)]

Department of Computer Science, Faculty of Science,
Khon Kaen University, Khon Kaen, Thailand
wpaweena@kku.ac.th

Abstract. Enterprise resource planning systems (ERP) are increasingly being adopted by organizations in developing countries. The objective of this study is to understand the processes and explore the key factors affecting ERP implementation in organizations. To derive the factors and to examine the situation of ERP implementation, this study conducts case studies of ERP implementation in private and public organizations in Thailand. The research offers an explanation of the differences in ERP implementation in relation to their organizational and cultural setting. The result from this study can be used as a guide for management in organizations planning to implement ERP to foresee and handle with such issues pertaining to the phenomena effectively.

Keywords: ERP system · Critical success factors · ERP implementation · Case study · Developing country · SAP

1 Introduction

The ERP system consists of different functional modules which are integrated by the software architecture and used by organizations to enter, manipulate, process, deliver data with the inbuilt business practices in real time across internal and external partners. The different modules are linked by the ERP system and the central database collects data from the different modules and makes it available for all business activities and functions. There are significant benefits to implementing ERP systems. They include improvements in managing human resources and payroll, customer service, scheduling production and inventory management [1]. The success of ERP in developed countries has stimulated developing countries to adopt this system into their organizations in order to compete in an increasingly competitive environment. Organizations in the developing country context pursue ERP systems for similar reasons to organizations in the developed countries: mainly to support their growth beyond what their previous in-house developed systems allowed and to stay competitive with other organizations globally.

However, using an off-the-shelf solution from a developed country in a developing country will often result in large design-reality gaps [2–5]. This is due to many factors, such as differences in working cultures, skill sets, access to technology and relevant

© Springer International Publishing AG 2017
F. Piazolo et al. (Eds.): ERP Future 2016, LNBIP 285, pp. 3–16, 2017.
DOI: 10.1007/978-3-319-58801-8_1

infrastructure [6, 7]. Many difficulties have been faced when implementing and using western technologies, management processes, information systems methods and information systems techniques in developing countries [8–10]. An ERP system is more than the use of stand-alone pre-written software; it is a change management initiative, which encompasses a view of business processes across the whole organization, requiring careful management of the associate human factors. The combined effects of process and cultural changes in ERP projects can create serious negative effects on user attitude. Harmonization of business processes and organizational structures are challenging due to language differences, differences in legal systems, differences in business practices from one culture to the other and differences in business culture with regard to management authority, openness, formality, and control mechanisms [4, 8, 11, 12].

Researchers suggested that language, culture, politics, government regulations, management style, and labor skills impact various ERP implementation practices in different countries [13–15]. Most studies on ERP systems use have been conducted in Western countries whose environments are similar to those where the systems were created. Furthermore, there is limited knowledge on ERP being used in developing Asian countries. Previous research suggests that companies in Thailand lags behind other countries in introducing new technologies and Thai users had a negative attitude towards the acceptance of new technology [16]. The examination of the cases of ERP adoption in Thai organizations also reveals that factors such as social influence and organizational support impact individual adoption [17]. Currently, there is limited knowledge on ERP system use in Thailand [18]. Therefore, these limitations will need to be borne in mind when considering the potential cultural impact on the use of information systems, particularly ERP systems. The current study intends to understand the key factors affecting ERP implementation in organizations in Thailand, a context that is different from where the ERP has been developed.

2   Literature Review

ERP systems have benefits due to the standard business process and integrated functions, but there are also a number of drawbacks. Implementing ERP systems is considered a complex project which requires a lot of investments in capital and human resources. Because of the large scale integration that takes place in any ERP implementation, the implementation project becomes highly complex and inter-dependent. An ERP System is one of the most complex information systems to implement because these systems can touch practically every employee and process in an organization. Organizations implementing these systems face both technical and behavioral challenges that are quite complex and fused together. Implementing these systems means having to change business processes and invest significant effort in training employees.

Major implementation challenges that have been highlighted in the literature include a lack of personnel skilled in ERP, cultural issues, training, technical complexity, organizational resistance to change, and difficulty in interfacing with legacy existing systems [10, 14, 19]. Other challenges are midstream changes in project scope, the misalignment between the system features and organizational requirements, project leadership, and a lack of resources [1]. Implementation of ERP systems dramatically changes the work environment because these systems are integrative and information intensive. The systems also enforce a shift from a functional to a process focus in the organization leading to wide-scale changes in the organization. Managing organizational change has been considered as a key challenge in implementing ERP systems.

Recently, the theme of ERP failures, especially in developing countries, has been a major discussion topic and it is argued that the organizational culture plays an important role while using ERP systems [5, 9, 10]. There has been an increase in reported ERP failures, suggesting that the issues are not just technical, but encompass wider behavioral factors and that the organization's culture and structure have a significant effect upon the implementation [9, 20–22]. The basic argument is that the business practices embedded in western-based ERP software are likely to reflect US and European organizational and national cultures, so when such systems are implemented in developing countries, problems may be experienced due to mismatch between cultural assumptions and practices embedded in the system and those in the client organization. It is of interest for researchers in organizational behavior to explore the factors underlying this phenomenon.

Most research conducted on ERP systems has been undertaken in organizations in developed Western countries whose environments are similar to those where the systems were created. There has been very little research conducted concerning ERP being used in organizations in developing countries. Previous research pointed out that business process reengineering (BPR) associated with radical changes were perceived differently in Asian and Western cultures [23]. In contrast to the Western cultures, the Thai culture is more past-oriented, reactive, and reluctant to conduct organizational transformations. Accordingly, the Thai culture must be taken into account when investigating ERP implementation issues in Thailand.

3 Methodology

The study used an explorative case studies approach, which provides a robust and rigorous ground for quality research derived from the corroboration of multiples sources of evidence [24, 25]. Case studies approach was appropriate as it enabled the researcher to gather contextual information on organizational structures—some of which were specific to the organization and others that arose from the organization's external environment. Multiple case studies were adopted, as they allowed the researcher to conduct a cross case comparative analysis for understanding similarities and differences in the ERP implementation process in organizations. The multiple case study methodology also gave the researcher more confidence in the findings by allowing the researcher to look at a wide range of similar and contrasting cases. A variety of data sources—interviews, observations, documents, and seminars—was sought to increase the reliability of the results. The principle of theoretical sampling has guided the case study selection based on the likelihood that they offer stronger theoretical insights [26].

Data were collected primarily through interviews, observations, and document analysis. When available documents related to each organization and the implementation project, such as mission statements, feasibility studies, reports, meeting minutes, project plans, user manuals, etc., were reviewed. Interviews were conducted with key players in the ERP implementation projects including members of the top management, functional area representatives, information technology (IT) professionals and end-users. The semi-structured interviews were conducted with 60 participants: 30 interviews at each organization. The interviews lasted from 50 min to three hours. One-on-one interviews were supplemented by multi-participant discussions where possible. All interviews were recorded and fully transcribed. Interviews typically began with generic questions allowing users to express their opinions before moving to more specific questioning to ensure that data from each case covered similar areas, thus allowing cross-case comparison, data collection ceased at the point of data saturation [27]. This study adopted an inductive approach, and accordingly, did not specify theory a priori to guide the data collection and analysis. Rather, relevant theories were investigated as data were analyzed.

4 Case Studies

Two organizations in Thailand, which have mandated the use of SAP, provide the empirical grounding for this study. The first case study is Thai-owned private organization and in the paper is referred to as SunCo. The second is in the public organization, here given the pseudonym MoonCo. The comparison between public and private organizations helps in identifying the challenges resulting from the organizational differences. Both organizations were using the SAP R/3 ERP system, version 7.0.

4.1 Case 1: SunCo

SunCo is a private company. It consists of three core businesses that operate in food, retail and distribution. Over the years, the organization has expanded its operation to several branches located in suburbs Bangkok. The management of the organization decided to terminate numerous legacy systems due to their obsolete functions and platforms that could not manage its whole business. The organization has attempted to make use of ERP system to support its back-office operation serving financial and supply chain activities. The organization has attempted to reengineer and reinforce its business through ERP system. In other words, SunCo took advantage of the introduction of a new IS as an opportunity for organizational change.

The ERP Implementation Project at SunCo
The ERP project planning started in late 2014. The implementation took place between 2014 and 2015. The system went live in 2015. During the initiation stage, multiple ERP software packages were screened and the best-fit solution was selected by comparing these packages in terms of solution cost, software capabilities, and vendor experience in the food industry. The selection process took four months approximately. In facilitating the project management, a steering committee comprising CEO and directors from related departments such as purchasing, accounting and finance and a project manager

were identified when the project was initiated. The steering team played an important role in planning and finalizing key decisions relating to project implementation.

The goals and objectives of the project and project participants were set up. The working team was divided into two main groups. The first one was an ERP vendor team comprising of consultants who played an important role in planning and implementing the steps and procedures necessary for the project. The other was the team comprising of IT staffs and key users from each department. Business requirements were gathered taking 6–7 weeks approximately. After that, the ERP vendor identified the gaps that existed between system capabilities and given requirements. Then, the steering committee finalized program customization and business process redesign. In this case, the management preferred process reengineering rather than the customization. After the system was tested for user acceptance, the data from the old system were transferred to the new one.

After the ERP system was installed, training sessions were conducted by the ERP vendor. Two levels of training were provided – ordinary user training for those entering daily transactions, and key user training for those who were intended to be acted as trainers and helped the end users when the system went live. However, many users complained that the training classes were not enough and too basic comparing to the real practice. In addition to the training, a manual was also provided to employees. However, users mentioned that the manual was too long for them and was in English, so they never bothered to open it after the training sessions. As one participant stated, *"I was so nervous to use the new ERP system because it was more complicated than expected. If I did some mistakes, others' work might be affected by my action. Also, the training class could not help much…real practice is not that easy"*.

The organization faced several severe challenges after go-live. Users were unable to carry out many of their system-dependent day-to-day activities. Also, some respondents argued that the complexity of system deterred their work paces. In some cases, what had been a simple ten minute process with the legacy system became an hour long struggle for employees as the incomplete configuration of the process in the ERP system. Consequently, they had adopted manual work-around to get the work done. In many cases, the amount of time required to perform transactions was ten times longer than required to do the same transactions with the legacy systems. The users, in some cases, required to navigate through 8-10 screens to complete a transaction that was available on a single screen in the legacy system. Combining these issues with the change of workflow, users felt confused and were unable to use the new system effectively. The users were frustrated by the learning curve and the efforts required changing to the new systems. The ERP support team, as well, felt stressed due to their inability to handle too many complaints and a heavy backlog of work.

SunCo had several challenges after the system go-live; however, the whole team was engaged to address issues that surfaced. The organization initiated several change management initiatives along with efforts to improve and fix the systems so end users could regain confidence in the ERP systems. Some of the key initiatives taken by the organization to increase system utilization included special training programs, one-on-one training and peer-to-peer information sharing. The key users also provided SAP user manual which was translated from English into Thai for users. The critical issues were detected and resolved in a timely fashion. The implementation process in this organization was an interesting example of regrouping low morale project team and frustrated end users to bring a delayed, over budget, and out-of-control implementation project gradually back on track.

4.2   Case 2: MoonCo

MoonCo is one of the largest government organizations in Thailand. Like many other government organizations, it is the sole supplier of critical services to Thais. ERP adoption was motivated by a decision to replace aging legacy systems with advanced enterprise systems that could extend some of the best business practices built within them for providing better administration. Before using SAP, most business transactions were conducted through paper-based processes and Excel spreadsheets. SAP was viewed as a back-office tool used to facilitate day-to-day operations. In other words, the ERP system was used to organize record and control data.

The ERP Implementation Project at MoonCo
The ERP implementation project planning started in 2014. The implementation took place between 2014 and 2015. The system went live in early 2016. MoonCo had limited experience in undertaking a large complex system implementation. MoonCo was not well prepared for implementing ERP. The company's managers did not fully understand that implementing ERP involved BPR. The implementation was very high reliance on external consultants and configurations that did not represent the business reality. In many instances processes were configured with very little input from the business. The organization was so focused on the project phase and meeting the go-live date that they did not plan for the post-implementation phase. Consequently, the organization's work was badly affected and constrained in the post go-live period. Business units had enjoyed significant autonomy until this change and they resisted the standardization and reengineering required for ERP system. Apparently, the organization had grossly misjudged the importance of business process input in configuring the ERP systems and vice versa.

The ERP vendor provided trainings for employees before the system go live; however, users who attended the training classes complained that the training only focused on the technical aspects of the system. Many users complained that the training provided did not cover their work scope, which made they feel uncomfortable to work with the system later on. In addition to the training, the manuals were also provided to cover the training session. However, the manuals were in English. Users had difficulty in understanding the manuals because of the language barrier. Consequently, they never bothered to open their manuals again after the training session. As one participant recalled, *"I think the system made my live more difficult and training was not good. For SAP systems, I need customised training that is contextualised to my tasks. I need to understand both how to use the system and the new business processes"*. It also appeared that some managers resist using the system and consequently there was much less enthusiasm in supporting it. As one respondent mentioned, *"Even my boss did not use the system and he also complained about it. So, my colleagues and I did not care much about the system"*.

The SAP software package was not totally translated into Thai. The English words in the user interface confused employees. A lot of English words appeared on the SAP user interface, and the software's user help was in English. As one user stated, *"I was afraid to use the system because user interfaces were in English. I was kind of blind when I looked at it. When I did something wrong, error messages were in English and I did not know what I had done wrong or how to fix it. So, I just avoided using it"*. Many users felt that SAP generated reports at a lower speed than Excel spreadsheets. The finance and accounting report format that SAP generated was also different from the Thai government's requirement and incompatible with the Thai finance standards. The reports generated by SAP always had some poorly translated words that made no sense to users.

The organization faced several problems in implementing the ERP systems. The organization took several months to tweak and improve the system configuration and their IT infrastructure after going-live, before the systems could be technically stabilized. The organization also faced serious problems as employees lacked proper training on go-live and continued to use shadow systems based on Excel spreadsheets for several months even when the systems were technically stable and working properly. The new systems and their implications were not understood very well by the end users. The organization did not expect the issues that surfaced and were therefore unprepared to deal with them in a timely manner.

Implementation of ERP in the organization was a long and strenuous process since the organization could not have planned for changes in the environment. Some of the key initiatives taken by the organization to enhance technical stability included extending the contract of the system integration vendor for an initial operations period until the capabilities for support within the organizations were developed. The organization issued a stronger mandate policy requiring all employees to use the system and announced the KPI associated with SAP use to evaluate employees' performance. The organization also had to initiate intervention programs to increase system use such as special training programs and group training. The length of the stabilization period resulted from business requirements that were not fully defined during the project phase, lack of user involvement and ownership, and inadequate planning and monitoring of the post implementation phase. One executive in the organization explained that being more formalized, their organization had more intense bureaucratic procedures for approval of additional resources and project personnel and it affected their time to achieve both technical and process stability.

5   Analysis and Discussion

The key factors influencing the implementation of ERP system at the case studies are discussed in this section. The six key factors affecting the implementation of ERP system derived from the study include change management process, top management commitment and support, business process reengineering, training, language and organizational culture.

Change Management Process

Change management refers to the managerial strategies used to overcome workforce resistance to the operational changes resulting from the implementation of the ERP system [28]. It appears from the finding that ERP implementations do not succeed because top management does not estimate the effort involved in change management. Change management considers the human factor and the involvement of the people in the project whose support and cooperation are necessary for successful implementation of the project. A well-designed change management team is important to address the implementation risks so that the potential for implementation success increases. The role of change management is to make sure users accept and participate in the implementation of the project. The importance of management commitment and involvement can be visibly explained with SunCo as a key success factor for implementing such changes. Many respondents mentioned that the management closely looked after the implementation projects, which made it easy to implement such changes in the organization.

The analysis also suggests that the main focus of a change management team is education and training in the ERP implementation and they should be involved in the design and implementation of business processes. The change management process educational effort should also be about business process knowledge acquisition. The change management team should educate the users on the benefits of implementing the ERP system and time should be spent on different forms of education and training.

Comparing the two cases, it appears that the lack of effective communication and policy enforcement prevented employees from recognizing the importance and benefits of system usage, which consecutively results in the low degree of user involvement. The analysis reveals that strong involvement of people from the field is important in reducing the resistance to changes resulting from an ERP implementation. Different change management strategies are necessary to change the attitudes of different users and inform them of the benefits of ERP. For success of an ERP implementation project, change management should start from the initial phase and continue throughout the entire life cycle. Change management should create a support organization, which is critical to meet users' needs after implementation. The role of change management team would be to have top management commitment, communication and training during the ERP implementation.

Top Management Commitment and Support

Top management commitment and support was found to be relevant in influencing the success of ERP implementation. The analysis exposes that top management support in the form of commitment and communication related to the ERP system implementation encouraged employees to use the system. The relationships between managers and subordinates are very important for Thai people. Moreover, Thai people put much emphasis on social network and personal relationship in the workplace in order to attract and retain employees to work for the organization in the long run. Thais tend to rely on managers in decision making since subordinates highly respect their supervisors. The analysis also suggests that beliefs about ERP systems were influenced by the appropriate diffusion of information by managers. If managers supported their staffs to use the system, it was more likely that employees would perceive the benefits of the ERP system to support their jobs. By contrast, if managers did not encourage their staff to use the system to perform tasks, it was more likely that users would avoid using the system.

Top management must be committed to their involvement and should allocate valuable resources to the implementation project so that it will help focus effort towards the realization of organizational benefits and lend credibility to functional managers responsible for implementation and use. Top management should create a favorable environment by getting involved in solving disputes and providing a clear direction for implementation success and getting the desired results. As an ERP implementation project crosses a lot of boundaries, the top management should mediate between parties during times of conflict and anticipate any problems that might be encountered during the ERP implementation. Top management creates cross-functional meetings by bringing different stakeholders together in the implementation process so as to enable cooperation between the groups. Top management should always provide the leadership and necessary resources for the ERP implementation.

The finding also suggests that that support includes not just time and resources to get the job done, but also necessary personnel for the implementation. They should also provide the necessary people for the implementation and give the required amount of time to get the job done. Policies should be set by the top management to establish new systems in the organization and help in driving performance during the implementation. Top management should be involved not only in strategic planning but also be technically oriented.

Business Process Reengineering (BPR)

The analysis suggests that BPR is also a key factor affecting the implementation of ERP system. BPR is a critical success factor for ERP implementation as it is an enabler in the process renovation for the organization. Aligning the business processes to the ERP's best business processes is critical. An ERP system alone cannot improve the performance of the organization unless an organization restructures its business processes. It appears from the finding that one reason why organizations fail to implement ERP is that they fail to understand or underestimate the extent to which they need to reengineer their existing business processes in order to implement the ERP system. For example, Thai organization managers tend to rely on experience, intuition, and insights from personal connections to assess situations and make decisions. They might not readily believe that they should change their current way of doing business due to the ERP systems implemented. ERP system integrates the western management standard which causes clashes with the Thai culture. Thai organizations need to redesign their current business processes to make the ERP implementation a success. ERP vendors must help organizations realize that ERP is not simply a piece of system that is easily implemented, but it represents a totally new business process model.

The analysis also suggests that vendors need to spend more time explaining the embedded data requirements and processes to the organization, as they can result in incompatibilities between the ERP system and organizational requirements in terms of the presentation format and the information content of the output. Organizations which are implementing ERP should look into their business needs, legal and regulatory requirements before reengineering their existing business processes. Organizations should map their existing business processes with ERP practices during BPR for their business goals and objectives. Particularly, public organizations need to look into constraints that may prohibit them from using the delivered business practices. Organizations need to appropriately manage their reengineering process by allocating the required time before undertaking ERP implementation in order to improve the organization's performance after implementation.

Training

The analysis also suggests that training is a key factor promoting ERP system implementation success if it was carried out efficiently. Training refers to the process of providing management and employees with the logic and overall concepts of the ERP system. The main reason for training is to increase the expertise and knowledge level of the people within the organization. Educating the users about the new ERP system can help the users buy into the ERP implementation and help them understand the vision of the whole project. This will help in reducing their fear and anxiety about their jobs and result in less resistance to change from the employees. Training helps the users use the system and motivates the employees to accept the ERP system. Training during the implementation phase of the project help the users become comfortable with the system and in turn increase knowledge and expertise with the functionality of the ERP software.

The analysis suggests that user training that included both technical and business processes, along with a phased implementation approach, helped users overcome assimilation knowledge barriers. Educating the users and training them involves not only the specifics of the new ERP system, but also the processes and integration of the different modules involved in the ERP system. Through the training, users can have a better understanding of how their jobs are related to other functional areas of the organization.

The analysis also reveals that training should be given at all levels of the organization, depending on the needs of the employees. Training must be tailored to fit the needs of the individual organization, and must involve people who understand the business, the business process, and the integration of the ERP system within the business. It can be more effective if closely tailored to the requirements of each user group. It offers a good opportunity to help users adjust to the change that has been introduced by the ERP system, and helps build positive attitudes toward the ERP system. Poor training of end-users can result in lack of knowledge in how to use the new system, as well as how to maintain it.

Language

The language poses another cultural challenge to ERP implementations. The findings revel that users had difficulty in understanding the system screens and user manuals that are in English because of the language barrier. Many participants feel that they are not confident in using the system and cannot understand many things on the screen because its screens were all in English which represented a challenge for the Thai employees. The participants also point out that inaccurate translation results awkward Thai words and causes many confusions. The translation from English to Thai for all the user interface messages and system outputs is a difficult and error-prone job. In many cases, direct translations from English to Thai do not make senses to native Thai speakers. As a result, the users found the system relatively difficult to understand and use. Therefore, great caution should be taken to ensure that the ERP system presents understandable Thai. More specifically, ERP vendors should ensure that all the modules of their system are thoroughly and correctly translated into the native language of users, including user interfaces, user help files and reports.

Organizational Culture

The analysis also indicates that organizational culture plays an important role in the ERP implementation success. There are differences in public and private organizations' structure, decision-making process and governance. One of the main factors differentiating private and public sector ERP implementation is organizational culture, which can have significant effects throughout the ERP implementation process. The analysis reveals that there were fewer users who initially resistance to the system in the private organization compared to public organizations. At SunCo, the employees seemed to have a greater degree of organizational commitment and a strong belief in their organization's decision. Employees from SunCo recognized that ERP system usage was strongly compulsory. The participants revealed that the organization had very strict rules whereby employees were required to follow rules. Consequently, employees were afraid of losing their jobs due to lack of ERP system use. The organization also had a highly competitive culture reinforced by an up or out career path. At MoonCo, by contrast, as the government's human resource policies in Thailand allowed employees to reach tenured status after serving probationary periods of employment, so employees in the organization enjoyed job security. Additionally, there was no evidence that employees were afraid of losing their jobs due to lack of ERP system use. When the system goes live, many users avoided using the system and some users continued using the legacy system.

It is very difficult to integrate the different departments and identify the process owners of the departments in public organization. The ways the project teams are created in the public sector also differ from the private sector. Private sector teams tend to be small and focused; public organization teams tend to be large to accommodate people from many different sectors. The analysis reveals that public organizations in Thailand are more bureaucratic, and public managers are less materialistic and have weaker organizational commitment than private organizations. Leadership and top management at public organizations do not focus much on project implementation compared to leadership at private organizations. At private organizations, middle-level managers play a very important role in implementing ERP system with the support of the top management. Public organizations' business plans and visions of implementing ERP systems differ from private organizations, as the goals and objectives of implementing ERP systems differ. From the case studies, the public's main goal of implementing ERP system was to replace the old legacy system while the role of the SAP system was seen to be strategic at private organization. For successful ERP implementation in public organizations, the plan and vision should include the tangible and strategic benefits, costs and risks involved.

The analysis also suggests that ERP implementation success is positively related with an organization's learning and development culture and an organization's sharing culture. The chance of ERP implementation success increases if the organization's culture has employees sharing common values and goals. An established organizational culture with shared values and common aims of being open to change and having a shared willingness to accept new technology, will aid ERP implementation.

6 Conclusion

The aim of this study is to gain insight into key factors influencing the implementation of ERP system, with a focus on ERP projects in organizations in developing country. Using the case studies to investigate the implementation of an ERP system in private and public organizations in Thailand, the six key determinants affecting the implementation of ERP system derived from the study include change management process, top management commitment and support, BPR, training, language and organizational culture.

The study highlights the importance of contextual differences in organizations and shows how they affect the impact of managerial decisions with respect to the ERP implementation in the organizations. With supporting evidence, the study argues that taking contextual differences into account is important for the successful implementation of ERP systems in organizations. For example, public sector organizations cannot always rely on some of the very common practices used by private sector organizations in retaining their skilled employees. All public and private organizations need to have an approach to change management, but the methods differ due to the underlying culture of the public organizations. This study agrees with Wagner and Antonucci's [29] findings that public sector organizational culture is different from private organizations and has significant effects throughout the ERP implementation process.

Leadership and top management should be involved throughout the ERP implementation in order to see the project complete successfully. Top management support and commitment does not end with initiation and pre-implementation but also must extend to the post implementation of the ERP project. The implementation of ERP must be viewed by top management as a transformation in the way the organization does business. Top management should publicly and explicitly identify the ERP project as a top priority and align the project with strategic business goals. For successful implementation, top management should monitor the implementation and provide direction for completion of the project.

As ERP implementation success depends on the business process reengineering, which in turn depends on the participation of the users, the change management team should be efficient in gaining the confidence of the users to take part in the implementation. The change management team should focus on the importance of communicating the change necessary due to the implementation of the ERP system to the required stakeholders. The change management team should develop a comprehensive strategy with the required tools to communicate with the cross-functional stakeholders, so that there is least resistance to the ERP implementation.

This study supports previous research that organizations that implement ERP systems often fail to continue providing training and support after initial ERP use [30].

Formal training and periodic review sessions are needed to ensure that users stay up-to-date with the process changes. The study suggests that users should be trained and educated in their specified fields and also about the overall process and concepts of ERP. This would help the organization in making the users know how their areas are correlated with other areas in the organization, which can help them use the system more efficiently and effectively. End user training should not be treated as a one-time event during ERP implementation; it should be considered as an ongoing process of communication and educational activities.

The study points out that ERP are not just an information system; it is a new way of doing business. ERP system implementation cannot be successful without understanding the need for BPR. Since Thai people tend to be more conservative and resistant to change. Thai users have low technological capabilities to use ERP systems and have insufficient knowledge about ERP systems. The lack of confidence may also influence their learning curve and slow down the implementation process. Misunderstandings about the nature of ERP systems further negatively influences the relationship between ERP implementation and culture. With this problem in mind, ERP vendors should invest in developing their own localized service group to work closely with their customers. All these initiatives should be part of the ERP strategic plan that gives culture adequate consideration.

The paper provides valuable insights for organizations that are implementing ERP system by describing the impediments that organizations can encounter in their implementation process. Because of the high risks and financial costs associated with ERP implementations, this paper also helps practitioners in senior leadership positions better understand the critical success factors in order to more effectively distribute the human and financial resources and improve the probability of success of the ERP system implementation.

References

1. Davenport, T.H.: Putting the enterprise into the enterprise system. Harvard Bus. Rev. **76**(4), 121–131 (1998)
2. Heath, H., Cowley, S.: Developing a grounded theory approach: a comparison of Glaser and Strauss. Int. J. Nurs. Stud. **41**(2), 141–150 (2004)
3. Kouki, R., Poulin, D., Pellerin, R.: The impact of contextual factors on ERP assimilation: exploratory findings from a developed and a developing country. J. Glob. Inform. Tech. Manage. **13**(1), 28–55 (2010)
4. Upadhyay, P., Jahanyan, S., Dan, P.K.: Factors influencing ERP implementation in indian manufacturing organisations: a study of micro, small and medium-scale enterprises. J. Enterp. Inform. Manage. **24**(2), 130–145 (2011)
5. Sun, H., Ni, W., Lam, R.: A step-by-step performance assessment and improvement method for ERP implementation: action case studies in Chinese Companies. J. Comput. Indust. **68**, 40–52 (2015)
6. Dada, D.: The failure of e-government in developing countries: a literature review. E. J. Inform. Syst. Develop. Count. **26**(7), 1–10 (2006)
7. Dwivedi, Y.K., et al.: Research on information systems failures and successes: status update and future directions. Inform. Syst. Front. **17**(1), 143–157 (2015)

8. Liang, H., Xue, Y., Boulton, W.R., Byrd, T.A.: Why Western vendors don't dominate China's ERP market. Comm. ACM. **47**(7), 69–72 (2004)
9. Rabaai, A.: The impact of organizational culture on ERP systems implementation: lessons from Jordan. In: Proceedings of 13th Pacific Asia Conference on Information Systems, Hyderabad, India (2009)
10. Dezdar, S.: Strategic and tactical factors for successful ERP projects: insights from an Asian Country. Manage. Res. Rev. **35**(11), 1070–1087 (2012)
11. Hawking, P.: Implementing ERP systems globally: challenges and lessons learned for Asian Countries. J. Bus. Syst. Govern. Eth. **2**(1), 21–32 (2007)
12. Huang, Z., Palvia, P.: ERP implementation issues in advanced and developing countries. Bus. Process Manage. J. **7**(3), 276–284 (2001)
13. Sheu, C., Chae, B., Yang, C.: National differences and ERP implementation: issues and challenges. Omega. **32**(5), 361–371 (2004)
14. Dezdar, S., Ainin, S.: The influence of organizational factors on successful ERP implementation. Manage Decisi. **49**(6), 911–926 (2011)
15. Shah, S.I.H., Khan, A.Z., Bokhari, R.H., Raza, M.A.: Exploring the impediments of successful ERP implementation: a case study in a public organization. Int. J. Bus. Soci. Sci. **2**(22), 289–296 (2011)
16. Intarakamnerd, P., Chairatana, P., Tangchitpiboon, T.: National innovation system in less successful developing countries: the case of Thailand. Res. Policy **31**(8), 1445–1457 (2002)
17. Suebsin, C., Gerdsri, N.: Key factors driving the success of technology adoption: case examples of ERP Adoption. In: Proceedings of Portland International Conference on Management of Engineering and Technology, Portland, Oregon USA, pp. 2638–2643 (2009)
18. Vathanophas, V., Stuart, L.: Enterprise resource planing: technology acceptance in Thai Universities. Enterp. Inform. Syst. **3**(2), 133–158 (2009)
19. Rajapakse, J., Seddon,P. Scheepers,R.: Why ERP Systems Fail to Generate Intended Benefits in Developing Country Organisations. In: Proceedings of 17th Australasian Conference on Information Systems. Adelaide, Australia (2006)
20. Nandhakumar, J., Rossi, M., Talvinen, J.: The dynamics of contextual forces of ERP implementation. J. Strate. Inform. Syst. **14**(2), 221–242 (2005)
21. Rajapakse, J., Seddon, P.: Why ERP may not be suitable for organisations in developing Countries in Asia. In: Proceedings of 9th Pacific Asia Conference on Information Systems, Bangkok, Thailand (2005)
22. Rajan, C.A., Baral, R.: Adoption of ERP system: an empirical study of factors influencing the usage of ERP and its impact on end user. IIMB Manage. Rev. **27**(2), 105–117 (2015)
23. Robey, D., Ross, J.W., Boudreau, M.C.: Learning to implement enterprise systems: an exploratory study of the dialectics of change. J. Manage. Inform. Syst. **19**(1), 17–46 (2002)
24. Yin, R.K.: Case Study Research: Design and Methods, 3rd edn. Sage, Thousand Oaks (2003)
25. Eisenhardt, K.M.: Building case theories through case study research. Acade. Manage. Rev. **14**(4), 532–550 (1989)
26. Glaser, B.G., Strauss, A.L.: The discovery of the grounded theory: strategies for qualitative research, Chicago. Aldine, IL (1967)
27. Miles, M.B., Huberman, A.M.: Qualitative Data Analysis. Sage, Thousand Oaks (1994)
28. Stratman, J.K., Roth, A.V.: Enterprise Resource Planning (ERP) competence constructs: two-stage multi-item scale development and validation. Decis. Sci. **33**(4), 601–628 (2002)
29. Wagner, W., Antonucci, Y.: The ImaginePA project: the first large-scale, public sector ERP implementation. Inform. Syst. Manage. **26**(3), 275–284 (2009)
30. Kang, D., Santhanam, R.: A longitudinal field study of training practices in a collaborative application environment. J. Manage. Inform. Syst. **20**(3), 257–281 (2003)

Qualitative Analysis of Different ERP Evaluation Models

Christoph Weiss[1(✉)], Manfred Kofler[2], Johannes Keckeis[2],
and Robert Friedemann[1,3]

[1] Andrássy University Budapest, Pollack Mihály tér 3, 1088 Budapest, Hungary
christoph.weiss@andrassyuni.hu
[2] Department of Strategic Management, Marketing and Tourism,
University of Innsbruck, Universitätsstraße 15, 6020 Innsbruck, Austria
{manfred.kofler,johannes.keckeis}@uibk.ac.at
[3] Westsächsische Hochschule Zwickau,
Dr.-Friedrichs-Ring 2A, 08056 Zwickau, Germany
robert.friedemann@fh-zwickau.de
http://www.andrassyuni.eu
http://www.uibk.ac.at

Abstract. ERP systems help companies to manage their business processes. The simpler and more efficient the business processes in companies run, the more profitable these businesses can be. Therefore, the process of selecting and implementing an ERP system is an important success factor. The qualitative analysis of ERP evaluation models examines necessary phases and activities for selecting a new ERP system.

Keywords: Analyse · Business software · Criteria · Decision · Enterprise resource planning · Evaluation · ERP · Market information · Model · Negotiation · Project · Requirements · Selection · Solution · System

1 Introduction

An Enterprise Resource Planning (ERP) system is a business management software [1]. ERP software solutions usually include relevant modules for managing and executing business processes in a company such as financial accounting, controlling, cash management, human resource management, planning, marketing, customer relationship management, distribution, purchasing, manufacturing, service, maintenance, logistics, quality management, inventory management and so on. An ERP system helps various parts or departments of an organisation to share data, knowledge, reduce costs and improve the management of business processes [2]. Nowadays, ERP vendors and implementation partners offer roughly the same bundle of functionalities in their software-products: a set of application modules that fit together. Each module includes a variety of functions [2].

The ERP life cycle consists of three phases. These are acquisition, implementation and maintenance [3]. This paper considers distinctly of the ERP evaluation. Among the major phases of the ERP life cycle, the issue of ERP acquisition is important. The stage

© Springer International Publishing AG 2017
F. Piazolo et al. (Eds.): ERP Future 2016, LNBIP 285, pp. 17–25, 2017.
DOI: 10.1007/978-3-319-58801-8_2

preceding the implementation process presents the opportunity for both researchers and practitioners to examine all the dimensions and implications (costs, benefits, challenges, risks, etc.) of selecting, buying and implementing ERP software, prior to the commitment a large of amount of time, money and resources [3].

Many academic researchers as well as practitioners have worked internationally in the domain of software selection. Most of the proposed approaches are variants of the multi criteria analysis, aimed at defining the final value of every available selection based on a set of criteria [4]. The decision to implement a distinct ERP system may also be made due to strategic, political or economic reasons.

There are various ways of perceiving software evaluation; it may be about different parts of the software itself, its development process and its maintenance. Thus, software evaluation is not a simple technical activity. It is a decision process during which subjectivity and uncertainty are present with no possibility of arbitrary reduction [4].

The objective of ERP evaluation models is to choose "the right" ERP system, which includes the demanded requirements for an organization. Different evaluation models are available to support the evaluation process. Shakir [5] respectively to a Decision-Making Model including six dimensions (classic, administrative, incremental, adaptive, irrational and political) and describes the assumptions and the decision-making process for each dimension. As listed in the Appendix, several researchers developed individual evaluation models, used multi-attribute decision-making models or an AHP-(Analytic Hierarchy Processing) based approach to ERP. These models are structured in different phase sequences.

2 Methodology

The methodology approach is structured in two phases:

- Literature Analysis
- Qualitative Content Analysis

In the literature analysis, scientific papers in the domain of evaluating ERP Systems are identified and used as a basis to develop a new ERP evaluation model. 26 different ERP evaluation models have been identified (see Appendix).

In the next phase, all identified papers are used in the qualitative content analysis.

In this content analysis, sources, phases, activities and tasks are qualitatively coded. Identical or similar phrases are combined and derived [6] as shown in Table 1.

Table 1. Example word analysis

Source	Level	Phase	Original wording	Activity
Q037E01002	E01	Analysis	Examination of business requirements and constraints	Analyze requirements
Q054E01001	E01	Analysis	Requirement identification	Analyze requirements

Within the word analysis terms are summarized as shown in the following examples:

- "analyze" (analyze, check, determine, identify, verify).
- "define" (appoint, define, form, set up, organize).

Next the sequence of phases and activities is determined. A mean value is determined from the occurrence of the identified first and last phase or activities of the analyzed models. A further average value is given by the sum of the multiplication of nominations per phase/activity number, and the frequency of the mentions in this phase/activity, divided by the amount of nominations per phase/activities.

phase/activity	Nomination in phase	$\sum$	A	B	C	D

$\sum$: number of entries in the 26 papers
A: sum of (amount of nominations per phase * phase number)/amount of nominations per phase
B: average of phase numbers (phases including nominations)
C: average A/B
D: ranking (column C)

3 Analysis

The number of phases within the different ERP evaluation models vary between three and nine. In this analysis, only phases which are listed in over 25% of the 26 papers mentioned before, were considered. On average 5.42 phases are present. Table 2 shows the considered phases.

Table 2. Considered phases

Phase	Nomination in phases	$\sum$	A	B	C	D
Project initialization	1, 2, 3	19	1,3	2,0	1,6	1
Analyze	1, 2	10	1,9	1,5	1,7	2
Requirement definition	1, 2, 4	7	2,1	2,5	2,3	3
Market information	1, 2, 3, 4, 5	21	2,8	3,0	2,9	4
Assessment criteria	1, 2, 3, 4, 6	22	3,0	3,5	3,3	5
Selection	2, 3, 4, 5, 6	19	3,6	4,0	3,8	6
Evaluation	1, 2, 3, 4, 5, 6, 7	22	4,2	4,0	4,1	7
Negotation	3, 4, 5, 6, 8	8	5,1	5,5	5,3	8
Decision	5, 6, 7, 8, 9	12	6,8	7,0	6,9	9

Each phase is structured with a different number of activities. In this analysis, only activities which are listed at least two times in the phases mentioned before, are considered. In the 26 papers, these activities are called sub-phases or detail descriptions.

P1 Project initialization phase
In P1 ten activities shown in the following table are identified. The activities are typical project management activities such as project initialization, examining conditions and project planning. Moreover, roles and project members must be decided, like appointing a project manager, the project team, and the steering committee with suitable competences and knowledge (business and IT) (Table 3).

Table 3. Activities Project initialization phase

Activities	Nomination in phases	$\sum$	A	B	C	D
Draft the project	1	5	1,0	1,0	1,0	1
Define steering committee	1	3	1,0	1,0	1,0	1
Decide project start	1	2	1,0	1,0	1,0	1
Carry out planning	1	2	1,0	1,0	1,0	1
Constitute acquisition team	1, 2	3	1,3	1,5	1,4	2
Establish decision-making team	1, 2	3	1,7	1,5	1,6	3
Appoint project team	1, 5, 6	7	2,3	3,5	2,9	4
Define project objectives	2, 3, 5	3	3,3	3,5	3,4	5
Appoint a project manager	2, 4	2	3,0	5,0	4,0	6
Use employees with IT knowledge	1, 9	2	5,0	5,0	5,0	7

P2 Analysis phase
In P2 four activities are identified. In the analysis phase, the requirements and business processes are collected, analyzed and documented. This also applies to the functionalities as well as the hardware and software infrastructure or the software support. Furthermore, restrictions are analysed and a potential analysis is carried out (Table 4).

Table 4. Activities Analysis phase

Activities	Nomination in phases	$\sum$	A	B	C	D
Analyze requirements	1, 2	3	1,7	1,5	1,6	1
Analyze constraints	2	2	2,0	2,0	2,0	2
Analyze business processes	2, 5, 7, 8	6	4,8	5,0	4,9	3
Carry out actual analysis	2, 18	2	10,0	10,0	10,0	4

P3 Requirement definition phase
In phase P3, requirements (business and technical needs), target processes and scope are defined (Table 5).

Table 5. Activities Requirement definition phase

Activities	Nomination in phases	$\sum$	A	B	C	D
Define target processes	1, 2, 9	3	4	5	4,5	1
Define requirements	1, 2, 3, 9, 10	5	3,6	5,5	4,6	2

P4 Market information phase

In P4 needed information on suppliers, systems, customers and interview data is gathered and validated. Based on the results potential suppliers are identified (Table 6).

Table 6. Activities Market information phase

Activities	Nomination in phases	$\sum$	A	B	C	D
Conduct market analysis	1, 2, 4, 6	5	2,8	3,5	3,2	1
Identify potential suppliers	1, 2, 3, 4, 10, 11	6	5,2	6,0	5,6	2
Obtain information about systems	2, 5, 10, 12	4	7,3	7,0	7,1	3
Collect information	1, 2, 4, 5, 12, 20, 22	11	5,4	10,5	7,9	4
Evaluate market data	5, 21	3	10,3	13,0	11,7	5

P5 Assessment criteria phase

In P5 all valuation criteria and criteria attributes are formulated, defined and weighted. These criteria need to be assessed and released by the Steering Committee. The results are outlined in a valuation matrix (Table 7).

Table 7. Activities Assessment criteria phase

Activities	Nomination in phases	$\sum$	A	B	C	D
Determine assessment method	1, 4	12	2,5	2,5	2,5	1
Determine selection criteria	2, 3, 4	5	3,0	2,9	2,8	2
Weighting criteria	3	2	3,0	3,0	3,0	3
Formulate assessment criteria	2, 3, 4, 9,	2	5,5	4,5	3,5	4
Create valuation matrix	4, 6	2	5,0	5,0	5,0	5
Define main criteria for pre-selection	2, 10	2	6,0	6,0	6,0	6

P6 Selection phase

In the selection phase P6, the necessary selection tasks are planned, the selection strategy is defined and a preselection is conducted. The preparation of a mathematical evaluation and the tender (incl. questionnaire for suppliers and demoscripts for process workshops) is carried out. The selection of the selection itself is divided into pre-selection and the final selection. The results of the evaluation phase are considered within the selection phase (Table 8).

Table 8. Activities Selection phase

Activities	Nomination in phases	$\sum$	A	B	C	D
Carry out pre-selection	3	2	3,0	3,0	3,0	1
Prepare mathematical evaluation	3	2	3,0	3,0	3,0	1
Define selection strategy	2, 5	2	3,5	3,5	3,5	2
Perform selection	2, 3, 4, 5	14	3,7	3,5	3,6	3
Prepare a questionnaire for suppliers	2, 3,8	3	4,3	5,0	4,7	4

P7 Evaluation phase

The evaluation considers technical, functional, non-functional and financial perspectives. Data and criteria are evaluated manually or (detailed) mathematically (Table 9).

Table 9. Activities Evaluation phase

Activities	Nomination in phases	$\sum$	A	B	C	D
Carry out Evaluation	3, 4, 5	6	3,8	4,0	3,9	1
Carry out mathematical evaluation	3, 4, 5, 6, 7, 8	12	5,6	5,5	5,5	2
Discard unsuitable systems	2, 13	3	5,7	7,5	6,6	3
Carry out a detailed mathematical evaluation	7, 8	2	7,5	7,5	7,5	4

P8 Negotiation phase

In P8 at the beginning, negotiating elements are identified and the negotiation strategy is defined. After successful negotiations, a contract is finalized (Table 10).

Table 10. Activities Negotiation phase

Activities	Nomination in phases	$\sum$	A	B	C	D
Carry out negotiations	3, 4, 5, 6, 8, 19	9	6,7	11	8,8	1

P9 Decision phase

In the decision phase the proper system is selected (Table 11).

Table 11. Activities Decision phase

Activities	Nomination in phases	$\sum$	A	B	C	D
Make a selection	5, 7, 8, 9	4	7,3	7,0	7,1	1
Make a decision	5, 6, 7, 9, 20	8	8,3	12,5	10,4	2

4 Future Work

The qualitative analysis of ERP evaluation models identifies nine phases including specific activities. In the next step, the results of this study will be used to develop an interview guideline to conduct domain expert interview. The results of these domain expert interviews will be in the form of a qualitative analysis.

Appendix

Evaluation model description	Research methodology	Model origin	Phases
ERP selection framework [7]	Qualitative research and case studies	Adapted model from Stefanou [8]	3
A conceptual ERP procurement model [9]	Case studies	Own model based on review of the ERP literature	4
Our proposed assessment model (E-OSSEM) [10]	Use case	Own model	4
DEA Decision Making Model [11]	Use case	Multi-attribute decision-making model for ERP system selec-tion based on data envelop-ment analysis	5
Evaluation Framework [12]	Use case	Own model	5
Proposed evaluation and selection process [13]	Use case	Own model	8
ERP selection Roadmap [14]	Use case	Own model	4
Acquisition process inside the ERP life cycle [3]	Expert interviews, data analysis	Own model	6
Comprehensive ERP project selection procedure [15]	Use case	Own model	9
A recommended map to successful ERP system implementation and operation in China (Selection part) [16]	Empirical study	Own model	3
Comprehensive ERP system selection framework [17]	Empirical study	Own model	6
ERP system selection procedure [18]	Use case	Own model	9
Model of the ERP acquisition process (MERAP) [19]	Use case	Own model	6
ERP system selection procedure [20]	Use case	Own model	7
Framework for evaluation [21]	Use case	Own model	6
Methodology steps [22]	Use case	Own model	5
Steps ERP evaluation and selection [23]	Empirical study	Own model	3
Software and Implementer Selection Phases [4]	Use case	Own model	4
Procedure of selection flow for ERP system [24]	Use case	Own model based on SVM (support vector machine)	5

(continued)

(continued)

Evaluation model description	Research methodology	Model origin	Phases
ERP system selection flow chart – decision phase [25]	Use case	Own model	6
The proposed methodology for the selection of ERP system [26]	Use case	Own model	7
Procedure for optimal ERP software selection [27]	Use case	Own model	4
ERP Implementation methodology propose phases and description of phases [28]	Literature review	Own model	8
Vorgehensmodell zur Auswahl und Einführung von ERP-Systemen in KMU [29]	Interviews	Based on Hansmann and Neumann [30] and Pietsch [31]	3
ERP evaluation process [32]	Literature review	Own model	7
ERP selection process model [33]	Use case	Own model	4

References

1. Piazolo, F., Paa, L., Keckeis, J.: IT-embedded strategic management. Mittelstand Kompakt – Information im Fokus **2**(2), 24–27 (2012)
2. Perera, H., Costa, W.: Analytic hierarchy process for selection of ERP software for manufacturing companies. J. Bus. Perspect. **12**(4), 1–11 (2008)
3. Verville, J., Palanisamy, R., Bernadas, C., Halingten, A.: ERP acquisition planning: a critical dimension for making the right choice. Long Range Plann. **40**, 45–63 (2007)
4. Nikolaos, P., Sotiris, G., Harris, D., Nikolaos, V.: An application of multicriteria analysis for ERP software selection in a Greek Industrial Company. Oper. Res. Int. J. **5**(3), 435–458 (2005)
5. Shakir, M.: Decision making in the evaluation, selection and implementation of ERP systems. In: AMCIS 2000 Proceedings. Paper 93, pp. 1033–1038 (2000)
6. Mayring, P.: Qualitative Inhaltsanalyse (Grundlagen und Techniken), Beltz, 12., überarbeitete Auflage, Weinheim und Basel (2015)
7. Haddara, M.: ERP selection: the SMART way. Procedia Technol. **16**, 394–403 (2014)
8. Stefanou, C.: The selection process of enterprise resource planning (ERP) systems. In: AMCIS 2000 Proceedings Paper 418, pp. 988–991 (2000)
9. Poon, P., Yu, Y.: Procurement of enterprise resource planning systems: experiences with some Hong Kong Companies. In: ICSE 2006, 20–28 May 2006, pp. 561-568 (2006)
10. Houaich, Y., Belaissaoui, M.: New approach for ERP open source software evaluation and implementation. Int. J. Eng. Res. Technol. (IJERT) **4**(08), 151–157 (2015)
11. El-Mashaleh, M., Hyari, K., Bdour, A., Rababeh, S.: A multi-attribute decision-making model for construction enterprise resource planning system selection. Int. J. Constr. Educ. Res., 1–15 (2015)

12. Sabau, G., Munten, M., Bologa, A., Bologa, R., Surcel, T.: An evaluation framework for higher education ERP systems. Wesas Trans. Comput. **8**(11), 1790–1799 (2009)
13. Khaled, A., Idrissi, M.: A semi-structured tailoring-driven approach for ERP selection. IJCSI Int. J. Comput. Sci. Issues **9**(5–2), 71–80 (2012)
14. Pitic, L., Popescu, S., Pitic, D.: Roadmap for ERP evaluation and selection. Procedia Econ. Finan. **15**, 1374–1382 (2014)
15. Wei, C., Wang, M.: A comprehensive framework for selecting an ERP system. Int. J. Proj. Manage. **22**, 161–169 (2004)
16. Zhang, Z., Lee, M., Huang, P., Zhang, L., Huang, X.: A framework of ERP systems implementation success in China: an empirical study. Int. J. Prod. Econ. **98**, 56–80 (2005)
17. Wei, C., Chien, C., Wang, M.: An AHP-based approach to ERP system selection. Int. J. Prod. Econ. **96**, 47–62 (2005)
18. Karsak, E., Özogul, C.: An integrated decision making approach for ERP system selection. Expert Syst. Appl. **36**, 660–667 (2009)
19. Verville, J., Halingten, A.: A six-stage model of the buying process for ERP software. Ind. Mark. Manage. **32**, 585–594 (2003)
20. Zeng, Y., Wang, L., Xu, X.: An integrated model to select an ERP system for Chinese small- and medium-sized enterprise under uncertainty, pp. 1–20. Vilnius Gediminas Technical University (VGTU) Press (2015)
21. Teltumbde, A.: A framework for evaluating ERP projects. Int. J. Prod. Res. **38**(17), 4507–4520 (2000)
22. Hidalgo, A., Albors, J., Gómez, L.: ERP software selection processes: a case study in the metal transformation sector. Intell. Inf. Manage. **3**, 1–16 (2011)
23. Ganapathy, N., Raju, J.: Enterprise resource planning system selection by small and medium enterprises: an empirical study. In: Tenth AIMS International Conference on Management, 299–309 (2013)
24. Zhang, M., Zhang, Z.: ERP system selection based on SVM. In: International Conference on Networking and Digital Society, pp. 13–16. IEEE (2009)
25. Cebeci, U.: Fuzzy AHP-based decision support system for selecting ERP systems in textile industry by using balanced scorecard. Expert Syst. Appl. **36**, 8900–8909 (2009)
26. Hamidi, H.: Selecting enterprise resource planning system using fuzzy analytic hierarchy process method. J. Inf. Syst. Telecommun. **3**(4), 205–215 (2015)
27. Liang, S., Lien, C.: Selecting the optimal ERP software by combining the ISO 9126 standard and fuzzy AHP approach. Contemp. Manage. Res. **3**(1), 23–44 (2007)
28. Pacheco-Comer, A., González-Castolo, J.: A review on enterprise resource planning system selection process. Res. Comput. Sci. **52**, 204–213 (2011)
29. Leyh, C.: Implementierung von ERP-Systemen in KMU – Ein Vorgehensmodell auf Basis von kritischen Erfolgsfaktoren. HMD **52**, 418–432 (2015)
30. Becker, J., Kugeler, M., Rosemann, M. (Hrsg.).: Prozessmanagement (Ein Leitfaden zur prozessorientierten Organisationsgestaltung), pp. 329–366. Springer, Siebte, korrigierte und erweiterte Auflage, Heidelberg (2012)
31. Pietsch, M.: Beiträge zur Konfiguration von Standardsoftware am Beispiel der Geschäftsprozeßimplementierung und der Parameterinitialeinstellung bei der Einführung eines großintegrierten PPSSystems, Erlangen-Nürnberg (1994)
32. Goztepe, K., Cetin, S., Kayaalp, A.: Designing ERP software evaluation procedure for a governmental organisation. In: 15th International Academic Conference, Rome, pp. 338–344 (2015)
33. Bakås, O., Romsdal, A., Alfnes, E.: Holistic ERP selection methodology. In: 14th International EurOMA Conference, pp. 1–11 (2007)

Business Processes

A Fact-Based Meta Model for BPMN

Peter Bollen[✉]

Department of Organization and Strategy, School of Business and Economics,
Maastricht University, Maastricht, The Netherlands
p.bollen@maastrichtuniversity.nl

Abstract. Recently, the OMG has been working on developing a new standard
for a business process management notation (BPMN). This standard development
results in documents that contain the newest approved version of a standard or a
standard proposal that can be amended. It is our vision that such a standard document, that also serves as a specification for BPMN modeling tool developers could
benefit from a fact-based model in which the same domain knowledge is represented conceptually as a list of concept definitions (including naming conventions), a set of information structure diagrams and the constraints or business rules
that govern the instances of the information structure diagrams. In this paper we
will show precisely, how such a fact-based conceptual view on a standard document can be created, and we will show how a fact-based approach can improve
the completeness of a specification.

1 Introduction

In the 1970's and 1980's a long-standing discussion took place on the stance that IS
developers should have towards approaching IS specifications from a scientific point of
view: *data-oriented* or *process-oriented*. Over the past decade or so the discussions have
changed because of the emergence of UML in which technically, the data-oriented and
process-oriented aspects are addressed 'equally'. At the same time, though, the field of
IS specification has undergone a dramatically shift towards 'user-friendly' and 'busi-
ness-language oriented' modeling languages like SBVR [1] and BPMN [2, 3].

In recent years OMG has been working on a standard for a Business Process
Management Notation (BPMN), e.g. see [2]. Although the development and standardization of a new business process modeling language of such a major standardization
organization as OMG is welcomed by the scholars and practitioners of business process
modeling we think that the achievements in the field of fact-based conceptual modeling
should be applied to the BPMN standard documents as well. It is our vision that such a
standard document, that also serves as a specification for BPMN modeling tool developers could benefit from a fact-based model in which the domain knowledge is represented conceptually as a list of concept definitions (including naming conventions), a
set of information structure diagrams and the constraints or business rules that govern
the instances of the information structure diagram.

© Springer International Publishing AG 2017
F. Piazolo et al. (Eds.): ERP Future 2016, LNBIP 285, pp. 29–41, 2017.
DOI: 10.1007/978-3-319-58801-8_3

In this paper we will analyze the BPMN 1.1 standard in combination with rules and guidelines on how to model appropriate BPMN models as is illustrated in chaps. 1 through 6 of the book by Silver [4].

In Sect. 2 we will give an introduction to the BPMN 1.1 modeling constructs as given in the standard document [2]. In Sect. 3 we will give the BPMN meta-model for Silver's level 1 palette of constructs [4]. In the meta model we will also add the modeling guidelines and constraints that are explained in Silver's level 1 BPMN method and BPMN style [4]. We will use the fact-based conceptual modeling methodology [5, 6] to express the BPMN meta model.

1.1 Introduction to the Fact-Based Modeling Methodology

Fact-based Modeling (FBM) is a methodology for modeling domain knowledge on the conceptual level. It is named after its main concepts: facts and fact types. FBM is applicable for all verbalizable knowledge sources. A verbalizable knowledge source is a document that often is incomplete, informal, ambiguous, possibly redundant and possibly inconsistent. As a result of applying the fact-based knowledge extracting procedure (KEP) [7, 8] we can create a document that only contains structured knowledge or a knowledge grammar. We note that the sub-procedure that is needed to instantiate the elements 1 through 5 (of the KRM) is known as conceptual schema design procedure (CSDP) [9].

In the fact-based approach, the fact construct is used for encoding all semantic connections between entities. The 'role-based' notation makes it easy to define static constraints on the data structure and it enables the modeler to populate conceptual schemas with example sentence instances for constraint validation purposes. The fact-based modeling approach has its roots in the seventies and over the years a number of dialects have evolved, i.e. ENALIM [10], (binary) NIAM [11], N-ary NIAM [6], Fully Communication Oriented Information Modeling (FCO-IM) [12], Object-Role Modeling [9] and CogNiam [13]. The OMG business rule standard SBVR can be considered the latest fact-based dialect specialized for declaring business rules [1]. The fact-based 'dialect' that we will use in this article is a combination of CogNIAM [14] and SBVR [15] for the list of concept definitions and naming conventions and the expression of concepts, ground facts, fact types and business rules in structured natural language [16].

2   The Modeling of Silver's Level 1 BPMN Palette

In order to precisely show how a business data –or information model is needed to create well-formed and well-integrated BPMN models we will start with the introduction of the BPMN modeling constructs that enable us to model the 'happy path', e.g. those sequences of activities that will be executed if everything goes as expected without exceptions [4]. We will restrict BPMN at this point to those modeling constructs that comprise Silver's level 1 palette [4]: Pool and Lane, User and Service Task, (collapsed and expanded) Subprocess, Start Event, End Event, Exclusive and Parallel Gateway,

Sequence Flow and Message Flow, Data Object and Message Flow. For an overview of the basic BPMN modeling constructs we refer to [17].

'An *event* is something that happens during the course of a business process' [2, p. 18]. 'An *activity* is a generic term for work that a company performs...' The types of activities that are a part of a process model are: *process, sub-process* and *task*' [2, p. 18]. 'A *gateway* is used to control the divergence and convergence of sequence flow' [2, p. 18]. 'A sequence flow is used to show the order that activities will be performed in a process' [2, p. 19]. 'An *association* is used to associate information flow with flow objects' [2, p. 19]. '*data objects* are considered artifacts because they do not have any direct effect on the sequence flow or message flow of the process, but they do provide information about what activities required to be performed and/or what they produce' [2, p. 19]. In Fig. 1 we have depicted the graphical representations of the most important BPMN modeling constructs.

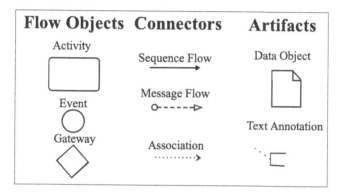

Fig. 1. Diagrammatic representation of most important BPMN modeling concepts

An activity is work that is performed within a business process. A *task* is an atomic activity that can not be broken down to (a) finer level of activity [3]. A *sub-process* is a non-atomic or compound activity that can be broken down into a set of sub-activities [3].

For a number of sub-types of BPMN modeling concepts additional attributes are defined. For example for the *event* modeling concept we have as an attribute the event type, that must either have the value: *start, end* or *intermediate.*

Gateways in BPMN are used to control the sequence flow in terms of convergence and divergence and a gateway has a number of attributes. There are basically three types of connectors in BPMN: *sequence flow, message flow* and an *association*. A *sequence flow* depicts the order in which the connected activities are performed. A *message flow* shows a flow of messages between two objects. An *association* is used to relate *artifacts* with *flow objects* and is mainly used to show the (data) *inputs* and (data) *outputs* of *activities.*

A *data object* is one of the three artifact types that are currently defined in the BPMN standard [2]. The 'incorporation' or 'leaving-out' of data-objects in a process model, is a way for some modelers to leave out 'clutter' [2, p. 93].

3 A Fact-Based Meta Model for the Palette 1 Modeling Constructs in BPMN

In Sect. 2 we have provided the definitions of the basic BPMN modeling concepts. In this section we will give an overview of the UoD that consists of the allowed BPMN expressions based upon the example that Silver uses to describe 'level-1' BPMN models [4]. This will be the starting point, for the derivation of a fact-based BPMN meta model by giving 'positive examples' that will lead us to the object types and fact types in the meta model. Furthermore, the modeling rules and constraints and the 'non-allowed' examples in the defining and practitioner's literature [2, 4] will lead to the definition of population constraints in the fact-based BPMN meta model. As a starting point for the fact-based analysis of BPMN example models we will use Fig. 2 (Fig. 5.7 on page 46 of Silver [4]).

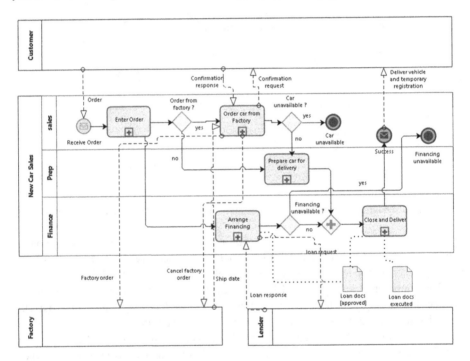

Fig. 2. Example BPMN model as in Silver [4]

3.1 The List of Concept Definitions and Naming Conventions

In this section we will group and synthesize the definitions of the main modeling constructs in the BPMN in line with the definitions as it can be found in the OMG standard document [2] and the modeling guidelines and naming conventions as they are recommended in Silver [4]. We create this list of definitions by scanning the standard and descriptive documents of BPMN for definitions and explanations.

We have taken these definitions and we have incorporated them, together with other definitions into our list of concept definitions in Table 1.

Table 1. (excerpt from) List of definitions for the BPMN standard, method and style

Concept	Definition
Activity	An activity is work that is performed within a business
Process	A Process is any [Activity] performed within or across companies or organization (OMG v 1.1., p. 32)
Process name	A name that designates a specific [Process] among the union of [Process]es
SubProcess	A SubProcess is a [Process] that is included within another [Process] (OMG v1.1, p. 287)
Task	A Task is an atomic [Activity] (Silver 2009, p. 27)
Task name	A name that designates a specific [Task] among the union of [Task]s within a [SubProcess]. The names should, preferably have the following format; VERB-NOUN (Silver 2009, p. 27)
User task	A User Task is a [Task] performed by a person, i.e. A human activity (Silver 2009, p. 27)
Service task	A Service Task is a [Task] in the form of an automated activity
Event	An Event is something that "happens" during the course of a business process (OMG v1.1, p. 18)
Event name	A name that designates a specific [Event] among the union of [Events]s within a given [Lane] of a given [Pool]

3.2 Identification and Naming Conventions

In this paper we will use 'local' identifiers for domain concepts. This means that we have to give specific naming rules for domain concepts. These domain rules should be in line with the definition of the name classes in the list of concept definitions. E.g., the name class *event name* is defined as follows (see also Table 1):

'A name that designates a specific [Event] among the union of [Events]s within a given [Lane] of a given [Pool].'

This means that in verbalizing instances of a(n) (type of) event in a BPMN diagram, we should use a compound identifier as follows:

'The Terminate End Event 'Success' within the Lane 'Sales' of the White-Box Pool 'New Car Sales'.

Another assumption, for naming conventions, that could have been chosen is to use 'global' unique identifiers for instances of concepts/object types. In most cases, however, this means that we need to introduce some form of abstract object ID that bears no single resemblance to the practice of naming these concepts in the subject domain itself. We note that the definition of our naming conventions includes the case in which 'global' identifiers are used ("global uniqueness implies local uniqueness").

3.3   Verbalization of Examples into Elementary Ground Facts

Now the list of concept definitions is complete, we will take the example that is depicted in Fig. 5.7 of [4]. Applying step 1 ('verbalization' or 'from examples to elementary facts') from the fact-based conceptual schema design procedure (while at the same time using the defined concepts and naming conventions from the list of concept definitions) [5, 6] will lead to the following fact verbalizations as SBVR ground facts (only a small subset of the verbalizations is shown here):

The **Black-Box Pool** 'Customer' has an outgoing **MessageFlow** 'Order' to the **Message Start Event** 'Receive Order' within the **Lane** 'Sales' of the **White-Box Pool** 'New Car Sales'.

The **Black-Box Pool** 'Customer' has an outgoing **MessageFlow** 'confirmation response' to the **SubProcess** 'Order Car from Factory'.

The **SubProcess** 'order Car from Factory' has an outgoing **MessageFlow** 'confirmation request' to the **Black-Box Pool** 'Customer'.

Figure 2 provides the expressions in a top-level process diagram. In order to be able to derive all relevant semantic associations between the concepts in the list of concept definitions for the level 1 palette we will add a second real-life example of an 'expansion diagram', as is for example given in Fig. 3 (Fig. 6-4 of Silver [4]).

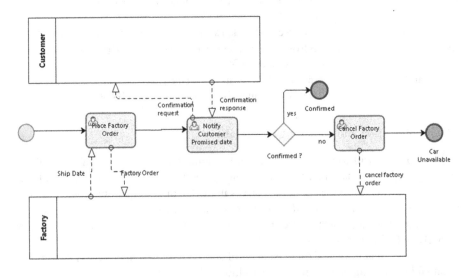

Fig. 3. Example expanded BPMN model as in Silver [4]

The verbalization of the content of the example in Fig. 3 leads to the following ground fact sentences (only a small subset of the verbalizations is shown here):

The **Task** 'Place factory order' within the **SubProcess** 'Order car from Factory' is a user task.

The **Task** 'Notify Customer Promised date' within the **SubProcess** 'Order car from Factory' is a user task.

The **Task** 'cancel factory order' within the **SubProcess** 'Order car from Factory' is a user task.

The resulting collection of sentences will allow us to reconstruct the original example using the telephone metaphor [6].

3.4   Abstracting the Ground Facts into an Information Structure Diagram (ISD)

In this section we will show the results of grouping the ground facts and abstracting them into 'fixed parts' (or verbs) and the 'variable parts' (or roles). The results of this transformation is a 'role-box' diagram that contains the abstraction of the ground facts and population constraints (see Figs. 4a, 4b, 4c and 5).

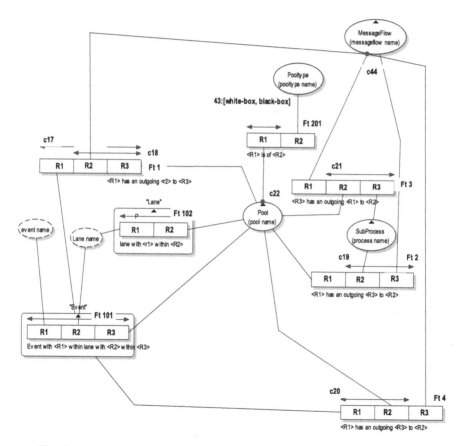

Fig. 4a. Information Structure diagram for BPMN palette 1 modeling constructs (I).

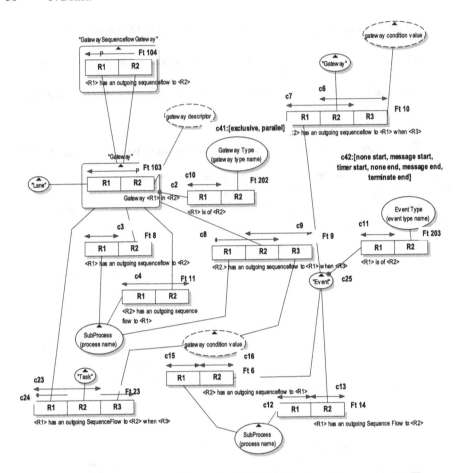

Fig. 4b. Information Structure diagram for BPMN palette 1 modeling constructs (II).

Note that we have given the fact types that are derived directly from the verbalizations in Sect. 2, a fact type number in the range from 1 to 100. Fact types that encode specializations of a 'super'- concept into 'sub'-concepts have been assigned a fact type number in the 200's. The fact types that encode a compound naming convention (see Sect. 3.2) for a specific concept have been give fact type numbers in the range from 101 to 199.

In Figs. 4a, 4b and 4c we have given the information structure diagram with the abstracted domain fact types, sub-type fact types and the 'compound' naming convention fact types and the population constraints. Because an information structure diagram can be considered to be a communication document within the domain of a business analyst we have introduced the naming convention for roles and fact types. In this way a domain ISD can be verbalized and analyzed, for example to see whether it complies to the meta model. In Fig. 5 we have given an excerpt of our example ISD for the 'BPMN happy path' including the population of the fact types.

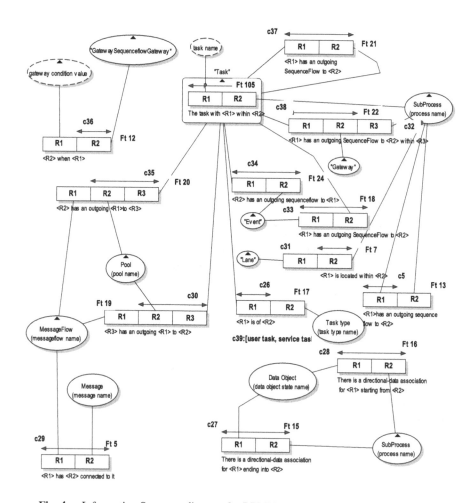

Fig. 4c. Information Structure diagram for BPMN palette 1 modeling constructs (III).

The content of the excerpt from Fig. 5 is equivalent to the following set of ground fact sentences from Sect. 3.3:

The **SubProcess** 'order Car from Factory' has an outgoing **MessageFlow** 'confirmation request' to the **Black-Box Pool** 'Customer'.

The **SubProcess** 'Order Car from factory' has an outgoing **MessageFlow** 'Factory order' to the **Black-Box Pool** 'Factory'.

The **SubProcess** 'order Car from Factory' has an outgoing **MessageFlow** 'Cancel Factory order' to the **Black-Box Pool** 'Factory'.

The **SubProcess** 'Arrange Financing' has an outgoing **MessageFlow** 'Loan request' to the **Black-Box Pool** 'Lender'.

If we inspect an allowed example in Fig. 5-2 of [4], we see that it is allowed that two different sequence-flows coming out from two different subprocesses can enter the same gateway. This implies that the potential uniqueness constraint on role R2 of fact type

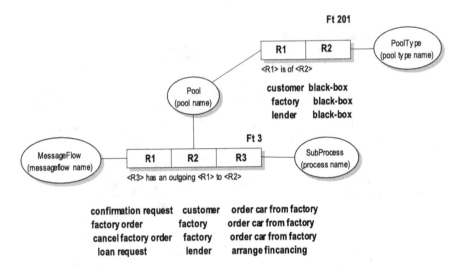

Fig. 5. Populated information structure diagram for BPMN example excerpt

Ft8 does NOT exist. After carefully inspecting many examples of BPMN models in the OMG standard and Silver's book we did not find a situation in which there's are two different outgoing sequence flows each to a different gateway. This makes sense because a token or process instance can only follow one path at the same time. However, this modeling constraint is very hard to 'trace' in the standard documentation and the text book we examined. So in Fig. 6 we have given an excerpt of BPMN model that is **not** allowed to exist.

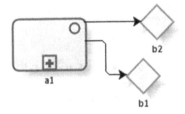

Fig. 6. Constructed non-allowed BPMN model for checking the co-existence of sentences (11) and (12)

Analogue to the derivation of the excerpt of the fact types in BPMN meta model we can create an example diagram based upon the following verbalization:

The **SubProcess** 'a1' has an outgoing SequenceFlow to **Gateway** 'b1'......
(sentence 11)

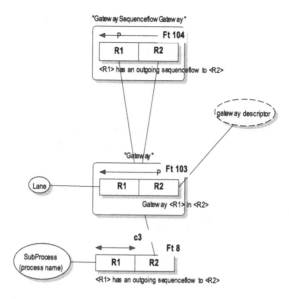

Fig. 7. Information structure diagram for fact type Ft8 including uniqueness constraint *c3*

The **SubProcess** 'a1' has an outgoing SequenceFlow to **Gateway** 'b2'......
(sentence 12)

Sentences 11 and 12 cannot exist at the same time, to depict this we have defined uniqueness constraint *C3* on role *R1* of fact type *Ft8* in the BPMN meta model (see Fig. 7).

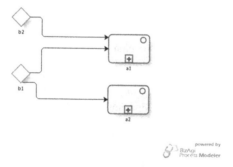

Fig. 8. Constructed allowed BPMN model for checking the co-existence of sentences (13), (14) and (15)

With respect to fact type *Ft11* all sentence permutations are allowed to exist e.g., the following sentences (13, 14 and 15) are allowed to exist in combination:

Gateway 'b1' has an outgoing SequenceFlow to **Subprocess** 'a1'.............
(sentence 13)

Gateway 'b2' has an outgoing SequenceFlow to **Subprocess** 'a1'.............
(sentence 14)

Gateway 'b1' has an outgoing SequenceFlow to **Subprocess** 'a2'.............
(sentence 15)

The diagrammatic equivalent expression of these sentences can be found in Fig. 8.

4 Conclusion

In this paper we have illustrated how a fact-based modeling methodology can help business analyst, standard developers, and tool-designers in capturing essential 'business rules' for applying (in this case) the BPMN process modeling standard. Although the standard document and a recent practitioner's text book were studied in detail, we have shown that essential modeling constraints were derived from (the absence of) allowed BPMN model examples. Although we have limited ourselves in this paper to the palette 1 modeling constructs for BPMN, the approach is fully scalable to cover the 'complete' BPMN standard or any other knowledge domain, as long as we restrict ourselves to 'verbalizable information'. The advantage of using the fact-based modeling methodology lies amongst other things in the strengths of using examples. As we have illustrated in this article, it is the 'semantic richness' of tangible examples or 'data' use cases combined with the information structure diagram (ISD). On a couple of occasions we have illustrated how the ISD in combination with allowed diagrammatic expressions 'expose' the domain rules that govern the instances of the BPMN modeling standard in terms of uniqueness and mandatory role constraints that are not explicitly documented in the defining BPMN literature.

References

1. OMG: Semantics of Business Vocabulary and Business Rules (SBVR), v1.0 OMG Available Specification (2008)
2. OMG: Business Process Modelling Notation (BPMN) OMG available specification v 1.1. OMG (2008)
3. White, S.A.: Introduction to BPMN. On demand business (2006)
4. Silver, B.: BPMN Method & Style. Cody-Cassidy Press, Aptos (2009)
5. Halpin, T., Morgan, T.: Information Modeling and Relational Databases; from Conceptual Analysis to Logical Design, 2nd edn. Morgan-Kaufman, San-Francisco (2008)
6. Nijssen, G., Halpin, T.: Conceptual Schema and Relational Database Design: A Fact Oriented Approach, p. 337. Prentice-Hall, New-York (1989)
7. Bollen, P.: The natural language modeling procedure. In: Halevy, A., Gal, A. (eds.) NGITS 2002. LNCS, vol. 2382, pp. 123–146. Springer, Heidelberg (2002). doi: 10.1007/3-540-45431-4_10
8. Nijssen, G., Bijlsma, R.: A conceptual structure of knowledge as a basis for instructional designs. In: The 6th IEEE International Conference on Advanced Learning Technologies, ICALT 2006, Kerkrade (2006)
9. Halpin, T.: Information Modeling and Relational Databases; from Conceptual Analysis to Logical Design. Morgan Kaufmann, San Francisco (2001)
10. Nijssen, G.: On the gross architecture for the next generation database management systems. In: Information Processing. IFIP (1977)

11. Verheijen, G., van Bekkum, J.: NIAM: an information analysis method. In: IFIP TC-8 CRIS-I Conference, North-Holland (1982)
12. Bakema, G.P., Zwart, J.P., van der Lek, H.: Fully communication oriented NIAM. In: Nijssen, G., Sharp, J. (eds.) NIAM-ISDM 1994 Conference, Albuquerque, p. L1-35 (1994)
13. Nijssen, G.: Kenniskunde 1A. PNA Publishing Heerlen (2001)
14. Lemmens, I., Nijssen, M., Nijssen, S.: A NIAM2007 conceptual analysis of the ISO and OMG MOF four layer metadata architectures. In: Meersman, R., Tari, Z., Herrero, P. (eds.) OTM 2007. LNCS, vol. 4805, pp. 613–623. Springer, Heidelberg (2007). doi:10.1007/978-3-540-76888-3_84
15. Nijssen, G., Hall, J.: SBVR diagram; a response to an invitation. Bus. Rules J. 9(7) (2008)
16. Bollen, P.: SBVR: a fact-oriented OMG standard. In: Meersman, R., Tari, Z., Herrero, P. (eds.) OTM 2008. LNCS, vol. 5333, pp. 718–727. Springer, Heidelberg (2008). doi:10.1007/978-3-540-88875-8_96
17. Bollen, P.: Business process model semantics in BPMN. In: Felderer, M., Piazolo, F., Ortner, W., Brehm, L., Hof, H.-J. (eds.) ERP 2015. LNBIP, vol. 245, pp. 31–45. Springer, Cham (2016). doi:10.1007/978-3-319-32799-0_3

Elicitation of Processes in Business Process Management in the Era of Digitization – The Same Techniques as Decades Ago?

Christian Leyh[✉], Katja Bley, and Sebastian Seek

Chair of Information Systems, esp. IS in Manufacturing and Commerce,
Technische Universität Dresden, Helmholtzstr. 10, 01069 Dresden, Germany
{Christian.Leyh,Katja.Bley}@tu-dresden.de

Abstract. For many decades, process models have built the basis for economically successful participation in the market. Companies are still faced with the task of identifying, defining and visualizing their processes, especially in today's era of digitization. In this era and due to more and more complex inter-organizational processes across corporate boundaries, the question arises as whether techniques and approaches for elicitation of processes in the context of business process management have changed or if the established techniques are still appropriate. Here, digitization could have significant potential to automate the elicitation of processes. To address this issue we have conducted a systematic literature review and identified the theoretical requirements for the elicitation of processes. Then, based on an interview study with experienced consultants, we compared the theoretic results with the current applied techniques in today's practice. Selected results are presented and discussed in this paper.

Keywords: Process elicitation · Business process management · Digitization · Process identification · Process modeling

1   Motivation

"It is not too much of a stretch to think we have entered a golden age of digital innovation. Owing to the 50-year march of Moore's Law, we have witnessed the creation of a relatively cheap and increasingly easy-to-use world-wide digital infrastructure of computers, mobile devices, broadband network connections, and advanced application platforms" [1]. This advanced digitization of industry and commerce as well as the further integration of smart objects, merging the physical with the digital world, seem to result in new fundamental paradigm shifts. These developments have crucial technological and manifold organizational implications, including drastic changes in business processes, implementation of new business models, increased requirements for business process reengineering, etc.

One of the most important challenges that companies currently face is the digitization of business processes and of the enterprise itself. They must join in global digital networking, improve automation of individual or all business processes, and reengineer

© Springer International Publishing AG 2017
F. Piazolo et al. (Eds.): ERP Future 2016, LNBIP 285, pp. 42–56, 2017.
DOI: 10.1007/978-3-319-58801-8_4

existing business models to gain momentum in digital innovation. Meanwhile, the progressive and steady digitization of society with associated changes has also arrived in the everyday life of enterprises. It has never been more important for enterprises to rely on IT-enabled capabilities and depend on a full understanding of information technology in general and in digital innovation in particular. A further aspect stemming from the ongoing digitization is the increasing complexity of enterprise-wide and inter-organizational business processes in combination with the variety of enterprise systems within the enterprise itself as well as along the supply chain. Nowadays, to stay and/or become competitive in the global business environment, companies must establish efficient and effective business processes in their own departments as well as with their business partners. Therefore, a certain process quality is necessary to ensure efficient company-wide and inter-organizational business processes. This has a strong effect on the prospective design of process management, especially on the procedures for process identification, elicitation and modeling. These changes and challenges are enormous and are no longer restricted solely to industry sectors that depend on innovative technologies for creating and selling their products or services. Nearly all enterprises have to undergo an increasing digital transformation to remain competitive in global markets. The areas affected by these changes are diverse ranging from the use of enterprise resource planning (ERP) or similar company-wide enterprise systems to achieve holistic support and planning of business activities throughout the company and across the company's borders, to the increased interconnectedness of classical horizontal value chains to a complex value network [2–6].

Only strategically intelligent businesses can remain competitive in the rapidly-evolving global, Internet-worked economy [7, 8].

Those innovative business models require more than ever before an active, correct and appropriate management, adjustment and reengineering of all business processes, not only in the enterprises themselves but throughout the value network.

Despite many past efforts toward system consolidation, businesses today struggle with heterogeneous and complex software landscapes. A tendency can be observed toward more architectural flexibility regarding enterprise systems and a certain rejection of strongly integrated approaches [9]. In this multitude and interconnectedness of the software landscape of an enterprise itself and within the entire value network of the companies, business processes become an essential and critical factor, since low efficiency, inconsistencies or errors within the process can affect many different systems and several companies.

In recent decades, process models have become increasingly important and numerous forms of notations and methods have emerged. Changes in consumer behavior, in the market structures and growing competitive dynamics have led to increased variants, elevated expenses and enhanced efforts of coordination and administration in all business area. The complexity of the enterprise has grown continuously [10].

On the technical and syntactic side there are many frameworks and practice manuals that describe in detail how companies model the underlying processes most appropriately and how they integrate them into everyday business. Reference models have also been developed that deal with the complexity of information and communication systems by using these models as a basis of off-the-shelf business software [11].

Identifying and collecting relevant information about processes is a crucial step in constructing a process model. However, identifying and eliciting processes in the given era of digital transformation is not addressed adequately in the literature. Processes are supposed to be given or known and problems arise in the field of optimization of existing processes [12]. Thereby, the focus of research was rather on the technique of modeling and less on the needs of the model user; this had far-reaching consequences on the model quality [13]. This aspect is surprising, since information from process elicitation is essential for the continuative design and optimization procedure of the respective processes. Errors that are made in the elicitation phase will lead to incorrect and inconsistent process models.

Therefore, the aim and contribution of this paper is a detailed portrayal of the process elicitation phase in the context of process modeling. This research compares theoretical procedure models and approaches with procedures and actions currently used and performed in business practice. In this field we focus especially on the needs regarding the ongoing digitization of the global business environment. Therefore, our main research question is:

Did the procedure for process elicitation change in the digital age or are the established approaches still appropriate?

We set up a study to gain a deep insight into the issues and challenges of process elicitation. For this purpose, five interviews were conducted to identify the influencing factors for ensuring a high quality in process elicitation.

To answer the research question, we evaluate the results of a literature study and discuss selected interview study results. Therefore, the paper is structured as follows. Following this section, we describe the key terms used throughout the research. Additionally, in this section we sum up the respective results found in the literature. We next present the interview study design (Sect. 3) and discuss selected findings in light of the main research question (Sect. 4). The paper finishes with a conclusion and an outlook for future research in this field.

2   Conceptual Background

2.1   Definitions

The term "process elicitation" is defined as follows for purpose of this paper [14–16]:

Process elicitation is one phase in the procedure of designing business processes. It includes the collection of process-related information, such as tasks, task support, times, amounts, etc. In this phase, various methods and techniques can be applied, which depend on the experience and number of people involved, as well as on the desired/necessary level of detail. In the context of process modeling, process elicitation often has an iterative nature, which means that phases of elicitation can alternate with phases of process documentation. Normally, the result of the process elicitation is a (process) model.

According to this definition, the aim of process elicitation is the collection of all necessary process-relevant information. This is achieved by appropriate management strategies, which include various methods, tools, etc., which are discussed in the following chapters in the form of recommendations.

Davenport [17] defines process identification as the first step of the process design. This identification is the draft, differentiation and exclusion of business processes. It also determines the activities and leeway in decision-making of the involved employees within the different processes [18]. Accordingly, the process responsibility is with the respective players. At this point it is assumed that process knowledge exists, which is displayed by [18]:

- An analysis of the defined business process.
- This includes both the structuring of a process (process design) and the bundling of processes to aggregates (process architecture).
- Knowledge of the respective players is a crucial prerequisite for an integrated processing of a business process and its integration of sub-processes.

However, the term "process elicitation" is not mentioned in this context by [18]. Based on [19] definition the step of process elicitation is located between the steps of process identification and process modeling. Figure 1 shows a graphical arrangement.

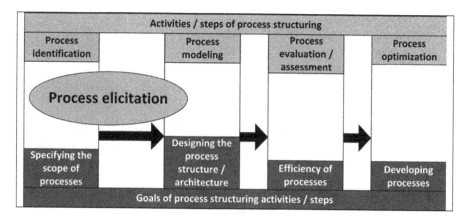

Fig. 1. Specifying process elicitation in the context of BPM (adapted from [20])

2.2   Process Elicitation – Techniques and Approaches

Below all information collection approaches in the context of process elicitation are listed (Table 1). We only list literature that explicitly suggests approaches for information collection, since many sources only mention the need for information collection or emphasize the importance of communicative aspects, but do not mention any collection techniques or goals in their designs. The results of the literature study show that there is a variety of non-automated approaches. Here, interviews and workshops are ubiquitous in information collection. Further, observations, questionnaires and the analysis of documents can also be seen as the main techniques. The information collection mix was explicitly mentioned in only one source. Automated approaches are rarely discussed. Here, process mining is one of the most often stated approaches in the context of process elicitation. However, this approach is not used very often since it is very complex and difficult to implement. Regarding the analyzed articles, the conclusion could be that an information collection mix represents the current practice of the approaches and, therefore, is rarely mentioned explicitly.

Table 1. List of different information collection approaches to process elicitation

Information collection approach	Literature (cf. reference section)
Non-automated approaches	
Observation	[14, 21–24]
Interviews	[14, 16, 21–27]
Questionnaires/written feedback	[14, 21–24]
Workshops	[14–16, 21–25, 27]
Web-based-conferencing	[23]
Document analysis	[14, 21, 22, 24, 25, 27]
Mind maps	[21]
Cause and effect-diagram	[21]
Route card approach	[15, 22]
Activity sampling	[22]
Time studies	[22]
Estimation	[14, 22]
Information collection mix	[22]
Automated approaches	
Process mining	[28–33]

The following section describes the arrangement of the most important information collection approaches according to Table 1. Therefore, the information presented stems from the references listed in the respective rows and are not separately listed for each sentence or paragraph:

An **interview** is typically used to collect detailed facts during a conversation. Depending on the hierarchical level of the interviewee, the level of detail of the information is high or low. That is, members of the company's board should be consulted for more strategic information, whereas the respective department employees can provide greater insight into the operational level. Prior to the interview, various conditions need to be clarified. This includes the selection of a professionally qualified interviewer, the selection of suitable interviewees, the clarification and definition of objectives and contents as well as the selection of an appropriate interview type. An advantage of interviews is that respondents are actively involved in the information collection process and thereby in the process design or process reengineering itself. This leads to higher acceptance of the activities as respondents feel valued. Moreover, this establishes a positive personal relationship, which might be useful in the further course of the process elicitation. The flexibility in interviews is also high, which allows for appropriate reactions to unexpected information and situations. Finally, intense discussions can be conducted, which may lead to a greater mutual understanding. The disadvantages of interviews can be seen in the required time (preparation, realization and documentation) and the required high level of commitment of all those involved.

Generally, **workshops** are used to identify requirements for new solutions. Regarding process elicitation, the solution in the case of the analysis of the current state would be the process model itself (and in the case of the to-be analysis analyzing vulnerabilities and thus determining opportunities for improvement and optimization). The common topic is initially distinct in the workshop, after which information and requirements need to be collected. At the end of the workshop, the further approach is decided, which, for example, could be an additional workshop. Following the workshop, the experts (e.g., the respective consultants) must prepare the results carefully and submit them to the participants for evaluation and voting. If deficiencies exist, either a follow-up interview or a follow-up workshop should be conducted. By the early involvement of various stakeholders the probability of the completeness of the results is increased. Analogous to the advantages of interviews, another positive effect is that the acceptance of the solution (the resulting process model) can be significantly increased through the active involvement of stakeholders. In addition, a mutual understanding is created, thus increasing trust between the parties. Therefore, the most important part of a workshop can be seen in providing a pleasant climate in order to build a trustworthy atmosphere. A major disadvantage of workshops is the scheduling, which can be difficult due to busy stakeholders. In addition, it is difficult to identify the "right" experts for the respective processes; this is, therefore, why preliminary interviews or document analysis should be conducted in advance. Furthermore, the qualification of the workshop moderator has a significant impact on the results since it may sometimes be extremely difficult to find a solution that is accepted by all participants.

Prior to studies in general, an extensive **analysis** of the relevant **documents** should be conducted. By analyzing various documents, it is possible for the collector to dive into the field of interest and to gather general information, which can serve as a starting point for further collection techniques (e.g., interviews or workshops). Basically, two types of documents are distinguished: (1) scheduled documents that are independent of the operational projects and (2) ad-hoc documents. Examples of scheduled documents include job descriptions, work instructions, etc. These documents are normally not distorted with respect to the aim of analysis, but may differ from the actual processes. Ad-hoc documents arise out of current events and often pursue a goal that may be related to operational projects. Examples include protocols and memoranda. Benefits of the document analysis are that this offers a wide information base and normally no falsification of the facts. Moreover the analysis does not interfere with the operational business; follow-up methods are enabled by a good analysis of documents in advance. The disadvantages are a lack of completeness, timeliness and consequently the real status of processes is often missing within the documents.

With the approach of **observations** the activities of individual employees are observed and the actual operations of a company are collected. As auxiliaries, accompanying notes requiring employee signatures can be used. This survey technique although beneficial, takes significant time and preparation effort, so its practicability is questionable. In addition, the observed employee can emphasize the technique as unpleasant or even as a threat, which complicates the practical procedure. Special methods can have a direct influence on the motivation of the observed employees and can help to reduce fears, but again require extensive preparation.

Questionnaires and written feedback are used when quantitative characteristics should be collected. The preparation and provision of the questionnaire is complicated, because no expert interviewer is involved, to actively support the procedure. Therefore, it is recommended to ask closed questions with a set of prescribed answers. Open questions are recommended when complex issues are given or suggestions are appreciated. Due to the intense preparation and in terms of a representative status, the number of respondents should be at least 20 participants.

Process mining is a business process management technique that aims to discover, analyze and improve processes by the use of event logs. The data of the respective process steps, which is recorded by an information system, is combined and displayed in its entirety. Process mining allows for implicit modeling and uncovers otherwise hidden process knowledge, thereby making it tangible and portable. This technology can be used especially when there is no formal description of the processes available or if the quality of existing process descriptions is questionable.

3   Interview Study – Data Collection Methodology

After providing an overview of literature-based aspects of the techniques and approaches for process identification, process elicitation and process modeling, we set up an empirical study to gain a deeper understanding of whether these techniques are actually used by practitioners and how this usage has changed in the age of digitization. Considering this aim and also in order to define best practices of process elicitation, we chose qualitative interviews as the most suitable research method. The approach of the "problem-centered interview" (PCI) by [34] has been selected since this enables the researchers to generate and verify new hypotheses at the same time. Especially in the context of the process elicitation, which is characterized by a high degree of freedom and by a lack of standardization, a quantitative approach was not seen as appropriate.

In order to detect and afterwards to use different selection criteria for interviewees, an Excel list was created. We searched different "I offer" tags on the German business portal XING (www.xing.com). By addressing this category, employees could be found who have the necessary knowledge to provide valuable information for our research aim. Furthermore, by using the search within the "Seeking" tags of individual employees, we were able to identify whether the person would be interested in an exchange of experience in the field of business process modeling.

A total of 20 potential interviewees were contacted in December 2015, of which nine responded within a period of two weeks. Finally, five persons (cf. Table 2) agreed to participate in an interview. Three interviews were conducted by telephone, and two were on-site interviews (one in Dresden and one in Berlin) in the first weeks of 2016.

The interviews were designed as partially standardized interviews using open to semi-open questions as initial starting points for the conversation. According to the PCI [34], an interview guideline was created prior to the interviews. This guideline included sample questions that were related to the different phases of process identification, process elicitation and process modeling. The sample questions were derived from the literature in combination with our own knowledge and experiences in the field of research. Further, the

Table 2. Categorization of interviewees

	Industry sector	Job title	Company size	Experience	Project goals (if specified)
I 1	IT-consulting (public sector)	Consultant/ business analyst	180.000 employees	7–9 years	Diverse (not specified in detail)
I 2	Public administration	Consultant	5000 and 150 employees; 2 projects	10 years	SAP implementation ISO 9000 certification
I 3	IT-consulting	Consultant	85 employees	6 years	Requirements engineering
I 4	Management consulting and IT	Consultant	100 employees	25 years	Diverse (not specified in detail)
I 5	Utilities	Business process manager	300 employees	12 years	Process optimization and audit

questions had a top-down approach and were summarized categorically. The interview guideline consisted of 17 questions. This guideline was sent to the interviewees beforehand to allow them to prepare for their interviews.

For a better analysis of the results, we recorded all interviews (the interviews took up to 70 min). Technically, the telephone interviews were recorded by means of a mobile app. The face-to-face interviews were recorded (with the consent of each interviewee) with a professional voice recorder to ensure the recording was loud and clear in order to simplify the transcription process. Afterwards, the interviews were transcribed for further analysis (resulting in about 48 pages of written text). During the transcription, non-verbal and para-linguistic elements and other elements that were not relevant to the study were excluded. The detailed transcriptions of the five expert interviews and the complete interview guideline will not be part of this paper, but can be requested from the authors.

The PCI stipulates reconciliation of the general data of the interviewee (I 1 to I 5) with the results of the interviews in order to recognize patterns and to formulate additional hypotheses. For this reason, information such as industry sector, or company size were also considered (cf. Table 2).

To analyze the answers given and information obtained, we followed a 3-step approach (adapted from [34, 35]):

Step 1: Individual analysis per interview: The individual analysis combines *content structuring* and *content summary*. The first step of this analysis is an iterative inductive coding process [36]. The respective transcription was analyzed with respect to the research question and important passages were clearly coded. Excerpts of interview transcripts that do not relate to the subject of the research question were not analyzed. This process was conducted iteratively: After analyzing the first two interviews individually, all existing codes were compared, adjusted and afterwards thus used uniformly. After the fourth and after the last interview, this iterative process was repeated. This ensured that the coding was uniform and comprehensible. We used MAXQDA software (http://www.maxqda.com/products/maxqda) to support the coding and the content analysis.

Then, categories were abstracted. As a result, three category levels were formed. In addition, those main categories were displayed in parallel in graphical form in order to structure the analysis process. With this, the principle of "openness" was reached according to [36], which advises not creating derived categories from the literature theory and fostering them within the empirical data, but rather the contrary, deriving categories from transcripts and comparing them afterwards with the findings of the literature. The final step of the individual analysis was to look at passages spoken linguistically to reshape them uniformly but without changing the key messages of the passages. To do so, we used the *Summary grid approach* as described in [35]. During this formal translation, different codings were adjusted one final time.

Step 2: Generalizing analysis: In this step, the results of the individual analysis were compared in MAXQDA using the function *summary table* and then exported as an Excel file. Too abstract or too specific statements (for example, referring to a single industry sector) were not converted because they were not very meaningful in furthering our research aim. With this step, we followed to some extent the suggested *intentional judgmental characterization* of the interviews by [34].

This procedure of generalizing analysis was also inspired by [35] who recommends both linguistic and substantive reductions (e.g., by removing duplicates or shortening long sentences). Therefore, the aim of this generalizing analysis is to extract all information from the interviews in a structured and universally valid method. With this, we avoided assessments of individual actions the respective interviewees made during different BPM projects because various methods coexist currently for conducting process elicitation and the approaches taken are strongly influenced by the respective project's conditions. Therefore, the result of the generalizing analysis provided a starting point for the next chapter where we compare the findings of the literature with the results of the interview study.

Step 3: Review phase: In the review phase, we checked whether our results still matched with the original material (the transcripts of individual interviews), or if any inconsistencies could be identified and needed to be corrected.

4 Comparison of Findings – Literature vs. Business Practice

Our studies (the literature review and the interview study) show that process elicitation is primarily associated with the analysis of the current state of the processes within the companies. It is conducted using techniques and approaches based on the specific project goals. Due to the high individuality of process elicitation projects, it is advisable to distinguish between process elicitation in narrower and in broader senses. The process elicitation in the narrower sense is focused mainly on the iterative steps/actions in which processes are identified, specified and documented (and/or modeled). In this aspect, process elicitation also addresses the different information collection approaches. Illustrating the last point, Table 1 shows the most commonly used information collection approaches. Interviews and workshops have particularly emerged as information collection approaches, as was also confirmed by the participants during the interview study. Here, a key finding of the practice is that formal and informal processes require different approaches. **Formal processes** can be identified and specified especially by conducting document analysis and later be re-examined by observations and/or interviews. Moreover, the lack of formal documents that is often given within each company is, to some extent, an indicator for problems existing within the company itself and, therefore, could lead to problems within the whole value network due to inconsistent or just inefficient processes. **Informal processes** in turn can be identified and specified solely through conversations (interviews and/or workshops).

A new finding arising in practice is that **interviews** are best conducted initially (at the beginning of the respective BPM project) with a process owner. This first information can be then particularized in more detail as the project continues. Furthermore, the term *detailed interview* was introduced by the interviewees. Detailed interviews are based on interview lists and interview guidelines that are gradually queried to ensure a complete survey. The high degree of individuality of the interview technique in general results in its outcome of different views in terms of actual interview methodologies. In combination with the findings of the literature, it can be concluded that an **interview-based approach** is seen as a very successful tool in terms of process elicitation. However, of special importance are the conditions such as time and place of the interview, which increase efficiency and correctness in interviews and, therefore, the success in the relevant projects.

Additionally, our research pursued the question of whether standardized interviews could be used as an information collection tool. The investigations have shown (especially the interview study) that structured interviews are not suitable for process elicitation since the interviewer is not able to refer back to or to freely react to unforeseen information, which is counterproductive in a standardized interview. Standardized questionnaires are partly used by consultancies, but most of the interviewees have a critical attitude towards them. A potential scenario for the efficient usage of such a **questionnaire** could be in industrial mass processes. However, this application/scenario is rather rare. It can be concluded that the skills of the interviewer particularly influence the success of interviews, so these skills should be supported and strengthened.

Additionally, it can be confirmed that **confidence and trust** plays an important role in interviews, which is why these conversations should be held in a private atmosphere. A maximum of four people should be involved in an interview, especially while identifying and specifying complex processes.

Beyond all information collection approaches, **documentation** is an important issue. Contrary to "typical" qualitative research approaches, the recording of interviews should be avoided in the context of process elicitation. The interviewed consultants mentioned a drastic negative influence of such recordings on the interviewed employees of the companies. Prepared interview guidelines and a division of the information collecting team in interviewer and record holders seems to be an appropriate way to structure and simplify the documentation process. In addition, the documentation has to be treated as confidential and internal until all parties confirm the content.

Workshops as an information collection approach were often discussed and described in detail both in theory and in practice. The importance of the preparation phase as well as the role of the moderator was clearly confirmed by the interviewees. Major differences exist concerning the execution of a workshop. The findings from our interview study show that the goals of workshops are reducing mismatches and aligning heterogeneous views within groups. However, in the literature, workshops are used to gather the requirements for a new solution. These views are not mutually exclusive, but rather are driven by a timely order. The gathering of requirements in order to find a solution is a goal that can be achieved through a workshop, especially at the beginning of the project. The matching of heterogeneous views will necessarily happen later in the project progression, particularly when large, complex processes are identified and specified and when many departments are involved. The procedure for conducting workshops described in the theory is consistent with the findings from practice.

The exact procedure was described in detail with regard to group composition. The findings describe a maximum group size of seven people to be optimal; otherwise, the "anonymity" factor in large groups gains significance. Next, the participants should be divided into homogeneous groups, although this is not absolutely necessary (depending on the objective of the workshop). For example, in a moderated confrontation, different views are deliberately presented together.

In practice, analysis of documents, web-based conferencing and observations are mentioned as information collection approaches as well. **Observation** was viewed critically in the literature, which could not be confirmed by the interviewees. Here, the advantages are particularly seen in the comparison of formal processes with reality, which is made possible by a neutral insight through the consultants. In practice, **web-based conferencing** receives a critical classification since most communication channels are not addressed and it is difficult to build a trusting atmosphere. Unanimously, a locally conducted process elicitation directly within the companies is preferred. The use of **collaborative tools** should be done only in exceptional cases. The usage of the information collection mix can be indirectly confirmed by the findings from the interviews. Important considerations are to be flexible during process elicitation and to choose the right approach for the respective situation.

The findings from practice are largely congruent with those of the literature. The procedure for project participants who are not experienced in process modeling is supplemented by the possibility of the initial usage of BPMN in a highly simplified form and expanding gradually as the project progresses. Furthermore, it is possible to use simple query maps. The modeling language is unanimously not seen as an essential factor for project success.

Table 3 summarizes the tools mentioned by the interviewees with and without database support (repository) as support for process elicitation.

Particularly important are the so-called **"coordination loops,"** which must be run through the entire process elicitation procedure. These loops ensure that all participants develop a common understanding of the processes until finally a solution is found that is acceptable for all (or rather most). In practice, the whole process elicitation procedure is often described as an "iterative procedure," where all responsible persons for the process should be involved. The result of the iterative process is a (result) model, which

Table 3. Overview of tools for process elicitation

	Tools	Literature	Practice
Tools without repository	Mind Objects		X
	iGrafx		X
	PowerPoint	X	X
	Visio	X	X
	Adonis		X
Tools with repository	BIC		X
	ARIS	X	X

is officially communicated within the company. Normally, two to four iterations are necessary in order to work out this model. At this point, the importance of the preparation phase is pointed out: by a good introduction into the project, sympathy and trust can be built quickly. All participants are motivated and, in the best case, wanting to participate. Especially during the iterative process, the information collection team relies on identifying and interviewing as many participants as possible that can be supported in a good project climate. Other restrictions in process elicitation are the typical constraints such as time, resources and money.

The most important step at the end of process elicitation is the **communication of the results**. Initially, the results need to be communicated internally to the project team and after acceptance by the participants; the results can be published throughout the company. In this way, a common level of knowledge is achieved. Particularly important is the branding of the (result) models. It must be clearly visible at all times, whether it be a current state model or a to-be model. Otherwise, irritation could arise.

In the case of different prerequisites, the "guided confrontation" within workshops is described as a solution. If there is an unclear task description, it is important to identify persons responsible for informal processes and to question whether they have the necessary process knowledge. Here, by means of a large "basic toolset" of the information collection team in terms of knowledge and experience, different types of problems and issues can be recognized or avoided.

The findings from the literature largely correspond to those in practice. Thus, the most important new findings from practice that were not treated or not treated in depth in the literature will be discussed in the following.

Generally, in practice, great value is placed on the **skills of the information collection team**. Most problems can be avoided by experience, mediation concepts, etc. It is advisable to acquire a process manager if there is a lack of skills and knowledge during process elicitation. This process manager should then be able to control the entire project in its complexity and provide the required approaches for success. **Communication** is the most important tool in process elicitation, which is why process elicitation projects, at best, should always be carried out on-site in the companies with all responsible parties. A useful extension represents web-based conferencing, which is suitable for distributed teams but used primarily in order to come to an agreement rather than to collect information.

The argument that experience can minimize problems is a fallacy because the focus is thus transferred from the problem to the interviewer. However, project success depends on the interviewer's basic tool set, for which he or she is responsible for the most part. Nevertheless, companies should be aware of the need not only to train its own employees, but also to analyze and to set up the project correctly in order to ensure the optimum utilization of employees.

5   Conclusion

In sum, we were able to show that process elicitation and the applied techniques in this procedure have not yet changed in the era of digitization. Although we could find a continuous increase in the complexity of inter-organizational processes and of business processes in general, companies, and especially consultants, do not see the need for new or adjusted tools (e.g., advanced tools for automated process elicitation) in order to define and describe their processes in the correct way. An ongoing digitization enables companies to combine and link workflows and to interconnect their value chains to complex value networks. However, we were able to show through literature review in combination with qualitative interviews of BPM consultants that the techniques and approaches of process elicitation remain the established ones that were already in use decades ago. The most common methods mentioned by the literature and interviewees were interviews and workshops. The question that arises at this point and that we will address in future research is why consultants and companies still see a higher potential in these approaches rather than in advanced automated approaches (e.g., use of data/ process mining or automated processes elicitation). One possible reason is the substantial effort that must be made to unite all involved parties in order to elicit their connected processes, especially considering the large complexity of inter-organizational business processes among the various partners in the dynamic value networks. In this context, trust and data protection could become a significant issue as the disclosure of internal organizational structures could mean a threat to a company's competitive advantage. In order to realize the full potential of the digitization but also to fulfill its requirements, it is the task of research and practice to create appropriate methods, tools or techniques to combine the advantages of classical tools with the opportunities that are offered by digitization and automation. Therefore, we will set up further studies, again qualitative interviews as well as large-numbered questionnaires to address and deepen this issue.

References

1. Fichman, R.G., Dos Santos, B.L., Zheng, Z.: Digital innovation as a fundamental and powerful concept in the information systems curriculum. MIS Q. **38**, 329–343 (2014)
2. Pagani, M.: Digital business strategy and value creation: framing the dynamic cycle of control points. MIS Q. **37**, 617–632 (2013)
3. Straub, D., Watson, R.: Transformational issues in researching is and net-enabled organizations. Inf. Syst. Res. **12**, 337–345 (2001)

4. Sambamurthy, V., Bharadwaj, A., Grover, V.: Shaping agility through digital options: reconceptualizing the role of information technology in contemporary firms. MIS Q. **27**, 237–263 (2003)

5. Wheeler, B.: NEBIC: a dynamic capabilities theory for assessing net-enablement. Inf. Syst. Res. **13**, 125–146 (2002)

6. Bitran, G.R., Gurumurthi, S., Sam, S.L.: The need for third-party coordination in supply chain governance. MIT Sloan Manag. Rev. **48**, 30–37 (2007)

7. Mathrani, S., Mathrani, A., Viehland, D.: Using enterprise systems to realize digital business strategies. J. Enterp. Inf. Manag. **26**, 363–386 (2013)

8. Sharma, S.K., Gupta, J.N.D.: Knowledge economy and intelligent enterprises. In: Intelligent enterprises of the 21st Century, pp. 1–10. Idea Group Publishing (2004)

9. Bley, K., Leyh, C., Schäffer, T.: Digitization of German enterprises in the production sector – do they know how "digitized" they are? In: Proceedings of the 22nd Americas Conference on Information Systems (AMCIS 2016), 11–14 August, San Diego (2016)

10. Becker, J., Kugeler, M., Rosemann, M.: Prozessmanagement: ein Leitfaden zur prozessorientierten Organisationsgestaltung. Springer, Berlin (2005)

11. Vom Brocke, J.: Referenzmodellierung: Gestaltung und Verteilung von Konstruktionsprozessen. Logos Verlag, Berlin (2003)

12. Gaitanides, M., Ackermann, I.: Die Geschäftsprozessperspektive als Schlüssel zu betriebswirtschaftlichem Denken und Handeln. http://www.bwpat.de/spezial1/gaitanides-acker-p.shtml

13. Rosemann, M., Schwegmann, A., Delfmann, P.: Vorbereitung der Prozessmodellierung. In: Becker, J., Kugeler, M., Rosemann, M. (eds.) Prozessmanagement, pp. 45–103. Springer, Heidelberg (2005)

14. Balzert, S., Kleinert, T., Fettke, P., Loos, P.: Vorgehensmodelle im Geschäftsprozessmanagement: Operationalisierbarkeit von Methoden zur Prozesserhebung (2011)

15. Fischermanns, G.: Praxishandbuch Prozessmanagement. Dr. Götz Schmitz Verlag, Gießen (2013)

16. Schwegmann, A., Laske, M.: Istmodellierung und Istanalyse. In: Prozessmanagement, pp. 155–184. Springer, Heidelberg (2005)

17. Davenport, T.: Process Innovation-Reengineering Work Through Information Technology, p. 5. Harvard Business School Press, Boston (1993)

18. Gaitanides, M.: Prozessorganisation: Entwicklung, Ansätze und Programme des Managements von Geschäftsprozessen. Franz Vahlen Verlag, München (2012)

19. Balzert, S., Fettke, P., Loos, P.: Plädoyer für eine operationalisierbare Methode der Prozesserhebung in der Beratung. Multikonferenz Wirtschaftsinformatik, p. 127 (2010)

20. Nüttgens, M.: Rahmenkonzept zur Evaluierung von Modellierungswerkzeugen zum Geschäftsprozessmanagement. Gesellschaft für Inform. eV Informationssytem-Architekturen, Wirtschaftsinformatik Rundbr. der GI Fachgr. WI-MobIS, vol. 9, pp. 101–111 (2002)

21. Gerstbach, I., Gerstbach, P.: Basiswissen Business-Analyse: Probleme lösen, Chancen nutzen. Redline Verlag, München (2015)

22. Schmidt, G.: Organisation und Business Analysis: Methoden und Techniken. Dr. Götz Schmidt Verlag, Gießen (2009)

23. Association of Management Business Process Professionals: Guide to the Business Process Management Common Body of Knowledge (CPM CBOK) (2009)

24. Koch, S.: Einführung in das Management von Geschäftsprozessen: Six Sigma, Kaizen und TQM. Springer, Berlin (2015)

25. Krämer, M., Görze, R., Hinke, R.: Geschäftsprozesse im Facility Management. In: May, M. (ed.) CAFM-Handbuch - IT im Facility Management erfolgreich einsetzen, pp. 69–111. Springer, Heidelberg (2013)

26. Jakobs, E.-M., Fiehler, R., Eraßme, D., Kursten, A.: Industrielle Prozessmodellierung als kommunikativer Prozess. Eine Typologie zentraler Probleme. Gesprächsforschung. Zeitschrift zur verbalen Interaktion **12**, 223–264 (2011)

27. Mayer, F.: Prozesserhebung. https://fritzmayer85.wordpress.com/2011/04/15/prozesserhebung/

28. Sarno, R., Wibowo, W.A., Kartini, K., Amelia, Y., Rossa, K.: Determining process model using time-based process mining and control-flow pattern. Telkomnika **14**, 349–360 (2016)

29. Van Der Aalst, W.M.P., Weijters, A.J.M.M.: Process Mining. Process. Process. Inf. Syst. Bridg. People Softw. Through Process Technol. **55**, 235–255 (2012)

30. Perez-Castillo, R., Weber, B., De Guzman, I.G.R., Piattini, M.: Process mining through dynamic analysis for modernising legacy systems. IET Softw. **5**, 304–319 (2011)

31. Centobelli, P., Converso, G., Gallo, M.: From process mining to process design: a simulation model to reduce conformance risk. Eng. Lett. **23**, 1–11 (2015)

32. Van Der Aalst, W.M.P., Rubin, V., Verbeek, H.M.W., Van Dongen, B.F., Kindler, E., Günther, C.W.: Process mining: a two-step approach to balance between underfitting and overfitting. Softw. Syst. Model. **9**, 87–111 (2010)

33. van der Aalst, W.M.P., Reijers, H.A., Weijters, A.J.M.M., van Dongen, B.F., Alves de Medeiros, A.K., Song, M., Verbeek, H.M.W.: Business process mining: an industrial application. Inf. Syst. **32**, 713–732 (2007)

34. Witzel, A.: The problem-centered interview. In: Forum: Qualitative Social Research (2000)

35. Mayring, P.: Qualitative content analysis: theoretical foundation, basic procedures and software solution. AUT (2014)

36. Lamnek, S.: Qualitative Sozialforschung. Psychologie Verlags Union, Weinheim (1995)

Towards Flexible Business Processes by Supporting Self-Organizing Groups

Christa Illibauer[(⊠)] and Christine Natschläger

Software Competence Center Hagenberg GmbH, Hagenberg, Austria
{christa.illibauer,christine.natschlaeger}@scch.at
http://www.scch.at

Abstract. Self-organizing groups are one of the most flexible and complex type of business process adaptations. The actors of a self-organizing group have to communicate with each other and adjust their activities in order to attain a common goal. A major advantage of self-organizing groups is the possibility to leave parts of the process flow unspecified but define the corresponding activities at run-time based on dynamic coordination. In this publication we summarize the requirements of self-organizing groups and provide an approach on how to use an unconventional process engine to support the participants of self-organizing groups to manage their tasks.

Keywords: Process adaptation · Self-organizing groups · Flexible business processes

1 Introduction

Self-organizing groups are one of the most flexible type of business process adaptations. The actors of a self-organizing group have to communicate with each other and adjust their activities in order to attain a common goal. Besides pre- and postconditions, formal constraints can restrict the coordination process. A major advantage of self-organizing groups is the possibility to leave parts of the process flow unspecified but define the corresponding activities at run-time based on dynamic coordination.

From this point of view, self-organizing groups can be seen as an extension of ad-hoc sub-processes, as defined e.g. in the *Business Process Model and Notation (BPMN)*, however, ad-hoc sub-processes have additional limitations and cannot be used as a substitute for self-organizing groups. While ad-hoc sub-processes currently are hardly supported by workflow systems, self-organizing groups are not supported at all, because they require extensive communication within the

The research reported in this paper has been supported by the Austrian Ministry for Transport, Innovation and Technology, the Federal Ministry of Science, Research and Economy, and the Province of Upper Austria in the frame of the COMET center SCCH. This publication has been written within the project *AdaBPM* (number 842437), which is funded by the *Austrian Research Promotion Agency* (FFG).

© Springer International Publishing AG 2017
F. Piazolo et al. (Eds.): ERP Future 2016, LNBIP 285, pp. 57–65, 2017.
DOI: 10.1007/978-3-319-58801-8_5

team. These problems have also been recognised by other researchers, e.g. Wulf
[1] states that "workflow system failed in the field of self-organizing" systems,
as the practice of cooperative work can hardly be described; he further indicates
that groupware offers a possibility to partly support self-organizing groups.

In this work, we identify general requirements of self-organizing groups and
propose an approach for handling such a flexible type of business process. We
base the approach on a formal specification of the execution semantics by means
of *Abstract State Machines (ASMs)* and, as a result, we demonstrate that the
tasks of self-organizing groups can be managed by using a proprietary issue
tracking tool with integrated workflow capabilities.

The paper is structured as follows. In Sect. 2, we provide an example of self-
organizing groups and compare their semantics to those of BPMN ad-hoc sub-
processes. We discuss the state-of-the-art in Sect. 3, present a formal semantics in
Sect. 4, and show how self-organizing groups can be supported using an existing
tool in Sect. 5. Section 6 concludes the paper and comments on future work.

2   Preliminaries and Motivating Example

The activity of writing an article for scientific dissemination serves as the motivating example of self-organizing groups within this paper. General requirements
(independent of each other and of equal importance) provide the basis for handling self-organizing groups and discussing BPMN ad-hoc sub-processes.

2.1   Motivating Example

Several academics work together in a research project and regularly publish the
results in articles. The organization of writing is determined by the participants
but the main tasks are predefined (see Fig. 1), as they have emerged from the
experience of the institute and the academics. The main tasks are to define
a basic structure, to find a person in charge for each section, to jointly write
and review all sections. Preparation as well as post-processing (review) requires
communication and group dynamics, whereas writing of a section principally is
done by a single, appropriate academic. A constraint defines that the person in
charge of a section must differ from the person reviewing this section.

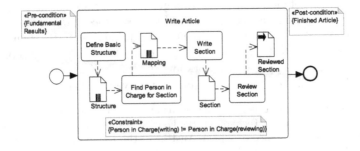

Fig. 1. Example of self-organizing groups

2.2   General Requirements

REQ-1: No Required Sequence Flows. In Fig. 1, a sequence flow between the tasks "Define Basic Structure" and "Find Person in Charge for Section" seems to be necessary; however, this would restrict the freedom of the actors as the structure may be changed later on. So, we claim that sequence flows typically do not correlate with the nature of self-organization (but we allow them).

REQ-2: No Start/End Events. In accordance with REQ-1, actors can start working with any task of the self-organizing group (if no further restrictions exist), which makes start/end events superfluous. However, we refer to the event concept to start an entire self-organizing group when the precondition is fulfilled.

REQ-3: Looping Semantics. Although it might be obvious to model tasks, which may be repeated (e.g. "Write Section" or "Review Section") using looping constructs, the semantics of self-organizing groups allows each individual task to be executed as often as requested by an actor (without any special highlighting).

REQ-4: Parallel Execution. We provide parallelism as the most flexible kind of execution unless there are formal constraints specifying an ordering on an individual basis, e.g. "Define Basic Structure" must not be executed simultaneously to avoid overwriting of results.

REQ-5: Completion. The overall goal of the academics is to finish the article, which is at the same time the post-condition of the self-organizing group. If the goal is achieved or in the case of a failure, all remaining tasks can be cancelled. In addition, there should be the option to adapt the post-condition at runtime to be able to flexibly react to changing circumstances.

REQ-6: Adding Tasks. A crucial factor for self-organizing groups is the possibility to insert tasks at runtime, which are not included in the process model. This is demanded as well by La Rosa [2] for "flexibility by underspecification".

REQ-7: Data Dependency. Within self-organizing groups the data flow (information flow) may be taken into account, as we stipulate to avoid sequence flows (see REQ-1). Therefore, the data flow may indirectly determine the control flow based on the availability of data.

REQ-8: Data Dependent Multiple Instantiation. In some situations an additional property of a task is required that indicates whether the number of instances depends on its input data, i.e. for data collections. For instance, when the task "Define Basic Structure" returns four sections, four instances of the task "Write Section" are required, which may be executed in parallel (see REQ-4).

REQ-9: Dynamic Actor Assignment. In some cases within self-organizing groups we need a concept to assign a specific actor to a certain task instance, which means that this certain task instance has to be performed by the given actor and must not be distributed to other actors.

REQ-10: Organizational Structure. The organizational structure within self-organizing groups has to provide for such flexibility to enforce actors to react to unpredictable situations [3]. This can be done e.g. by avoiding rigid bureaucratic hierarchies or allowing actors to ignore some constraints.

2.3 The BPMN Ad-Hoc Sub-process

The ad-hoc sub-process is proposed by the BPMN standard [4] as a set of activities whose sequence and numbers of executions are decided by their performers. A formal specification of its execution semantics is given in [5]. However, ad-hoc sub-processes can only be executed by a subset of existing process engines and only meet a limited number of the identified requirements (see Table 1).

Although the semantics of ad-hoc sub-processes is similar to those of self-organizing groups to a certain extent, a major weakness of the ad-hoc sub-process is that all comprising tasks must be specified at design time. In addition, some requirements can only partly be met by using the defined attributes. Further limitations of ad-hoc sub-processes are given by insufficient specifications.

Table 1. Fulfilment of Requirements by BPMN Ad-Hoc Sub-process

Requirement	Satisfied	Comment
REQ-1	Yes	Sequence flows may be omitted
REQ-2	Yes	No start and end events are comprised
REQ-3	Yes	the comprising tasks can be executed multiple times
REQ-4	Partly	*Ordering* can either be "Parallel" or "Sequential", whereby sequential execution affects the whole sub-process, which is too inflexible
REQ-5	Partly	Cancelling of remaining task instances is supported; however, *completionCondition* is rather rigid and thus not suitable for actors to co-decide when the process is finished
REQ-6	No	There is no possibility to insert an additional task at runtime
REQ-7	No	Data dependencies are not mentioned for ad-hoc sub-processes
REQ-8	No	Data dependencies are not mentioned for ad-hoc sub-processes
REQ-9	Yes	Dynamic actor assignment is provided
REQ-10	No	The organisational structure is not sufficiently specified

3   State-of-the-Art

Already from 1962, self-organizing systems have been investigated, e.g. by Ashby [6], Goldstein [7], or Serguendo et al. [8]. According to the categorisation introduced by La Rosa [2], the approach of self-organizing groups relates to flexibility by underspecification. Underspecified activities denote activities in a business process that are abstractly defined and not executable.

Hagen et al. [9] use the term "unstructured process", when the process model is not fully defined. They propose that neither rules for subsequent activities nor the potential activities need to be known in advance. Common to our approach of self-organizing groups is the focus on processes, but our intention is not to achieve an optimal process but to support different executions of the process depending on the current context.

Sungur et al. [10] provide an approach to support context-sensitive, adaptive production processes, which are able to be used within smart factories. This approach differs from ours in the sense that we do not use selection strategies but use data flows and allow user decisions.

Bucchiarone et al. [11] propose a framework for adaptivity of service-based applications, which allows underspecified processes to be automatically refined at runtime by taking the specific execution context into account. In contrast to our approach, they focus on service-based systems and not on business processes.

Pesic et al. [12] suggest declarative models describing loosely-structured processes. Although declarative languages are highly suitable for flexible scenarios, they are based on another modelling paradigm than addressed in this paper.

Further research on flexible business processes can be found in [13], where the major focus is on process adaptations but not on self-organizing groups.

Regarding tool support, Reijers et al. [14] point out that existing workflow management systems do not offer awareness of a situation and the flexibility to change. Wulf [1] investigates how the introduction of groupware into organisations influences existing cooperation patterns. He states that "workflow system failed in the field of self-organizing systems", as the practice of cooperative work can hardly be described. This article agrees with our experience that existing workflow systems are not capable of supporting self-organizing groups but groupware may be used to some extent.

4   Semantics of Self-Organizing Groups

We use the ASM method [15], a system engineering method with a rigorous mathematical foundation for developing systems seamlessly from requirements capture to implementation, to specify the operational semantics of self-organizing groups such that no room for interpretation is left. The formal specification is based on the *Hagenberg Business Process Modelling (H-BPM)* method [5,16], which we extend by a new type of activity to support self-organizing groups called *SelfOrganizingGroupTransition* (a small part of the specification is presented below) to address the requirements REQ-1 to REQ-9. REQ-10 is dealt within the actor approach of H-BPM [17], which provides a flexible role hierarchy and allows for specifying restrictions.

We plan to publish the complete specification any time soon.

```
rule SelfOrganizingGroupTransition(flowNode) =
    ActivityTransition(flowNode) where
  [...]
  forall node ∈ activityNodes(flowNode) with
      incomingSequenceFlows(node) = {} and
      incomingDataFlows(node) = {} do
    CreateInstance(node, instance, correlationInfo(instance))
  [...]
  if evaluate(postCondition(flowNode)) then
    DoSOGCleanup(instance, flowNode)
    else
      CreateAdditionalTasks(instance, flowNode)
```

5   Supporting Self-Organizing Groups Using JIRA

We now show how the tool Atlassian JIRA [18] can be used to support the actors of self-organizing groups to handle their tasks. JIRA does not support business processes as a common workflow engine would do; for instance, instantiation of (user) tasks must be done manually in JIRA or by offering methods which handle the creation of issues programmatically. In this way, the main activities can statically be predefined (e.g. as tasks) and at runtime actors can create appropriate sub-tasks. The sub-tasks can then be assigned to individual actors.

Another key difference between a common workflow engine and JIRA is that JIRA does not define sequence flows. A user can select and start a task of their work list using the JIRA action "Start Process" and complete the task via "Resolve Issue". After the completion of a task, a typical workflow engine would create an instance of the subsequent task and offer it to the assigned actor(s). In JIRA, just as with self-organizing groups, it is mainly up to the actors when they want to perform certain tasks.

Regarding workflows, several lifecycle states of activities, as e.g. proposed by the BPMN standard, can be mapped to states provided by JIRA. For the transition of one state to another, JIRA uses a built-in process engine. The JIRA states "Open" and "In Progress" relate to the BPMN lifecycle states "Ready" and "Active" respectively, just as the JIRA state "Resolved" relates to the lifecycle state "Completed". The failure lifecycle states "Failed", "Terminated", or "Withdrawn" may be equivalent to the JIRA state "Closed".

For programmatic support, JIRA provides the *Representational State Transfer* (REST) API that allows to access the JIRA environment and, additionally, provides a lot of classes that ease the access (e.g. the class *JiraRestClient*). As development environment we use Eclipse Java EE IDE for Web Developers Version Mars.2. Figure 2 shows some JIRA tasks and sub-tasks available for writing

WRIT-3	WRIT-1 / Find Person in Charge for Section	Unassigned	↑	OPEN	Unresolved
WRIT-2	WRIT-1 / Define Basic Structure	Illibauer Christa	↑	RESOLVED	Fixed
WRIT-1	Write Article	Illibauer Christa	↑	IN PROGRESS	Unresolved

Fig. 2. Tasks and sub-tasks in JIRA

an article for scientific dissemination introduced in Sect. 2.1. We only provide methods for the creation of the issues in JIRA but not for changing the states, as JIRA already offers good support for the actors via the JIRA GUI, which provides several actions (e.g. "Start Process", "Close Issue", and so on).

Discussion of Results. We showed that the tasks of self-organizing groups can be managed by using the widespread software development tool JIRA with its built-in process engine, as the tool supports distribution (assignment) of a single task/sub-task to an actor and provides different states for each task. In addition, the application scenario demonstrates that only the creation of tasks/sub-tasks, including the assignment to the actors, should be supported programmatically, as the participants are well supported by the tool for all other actions (like changing the status). Communication has to be managed by the participants themselves, i.e. the assignment of tasks to a particular actor already includes communication, as the assigner communicates what has to be done to the assignee(s).

In our company, a lot of projects are carried out and in most of them we use JIRA for issue tracking. Since in many of them scientific articles are written, our motivating example of self-organizing groups will frequently be applied in future to provide a much better support for the authors.

Table 2. Fulfilment of requirements within the approach

Requirement	Satisfied	Comment
REQ-1	Yes	JIRA does not provide for sequences
REQ-2	Yes	JIRA does not provide for start and end events
REQ-3	Yes	JIRA allows task/sub-task creation at any time
REQ-4	Partly	JIRA allows parallel execution, sequential execution must be handled by the actors
REQ-5	Partly	JIRA provides GUI actions, completion must be handled by the actors
REQ-6	Yes	JIRA allows task/sub-task creation at any time
REQ-7	No	Data dependency must be handled by the actors
REQ-8	No	Data dependency must be handled by the actors
REQ-9	Yes	JIRA allows actor assignment at any time
REQ-10	Yes	JIRA provides administration for user/group

An overview of which requirements, defined in Sect. 2.2, are satisfied within the approach of using JIRA for supporting self-organizing groups is presented in Table 2. The table shows that six out of ten requirements are fulfilled, two are partly fulfilled, and the users of self-organizing groups must be aware of the remaining ones (in particular regarding data dependency).

6   Conclusion

Besides other types of business process adaptations like context-based, actor-based, or preference-based adaptations, which we already investigated in previous research and whose results we have partly published, e.g. in [13,19,20], in this publication we concentrated on self-organizing groups, one of the most flexible and complex type of business process adaptations.

We first summarized the requirements of self-organizing groups and then specified their semantics using ASMs to guarantee that their executable behaviour is as expected. Furthermore, we provided an approach on how to use JIRA to support the actors of self-organizing groups in managing their tasks by either creating the necessary issues manually or by implementing a Java application that offers the corresponding methods. We also demonstrated the practical applicability via a scenario for writing an article for scientific dissemination.

In future research we will explore goal-based adaptations, an extension of preference-based adaptations to support flexible business processes with an optional actor profile. The actors can themselves adapt the process flow also with unspecified activities in order to achieve the defined goals.

References

1. Wulf, V.: Evolving cooperation when introducing groupware - a self-organization perspective. Cybern. Hum. Knowing **6**(2), 55–75 (1999)
2. La Rosa, M., van der Aalst, W., Dumas, M., Milani, F.: Business process variability modeling: a survey. Technical report, QUT (2013)
3. Coleman, H.J.J.: What enables self-organizing behavior in businesses. Emergence Complexity Organ. **1**(1), 33–48 (1999)
4. Object Management Group: Business process model and notation (BPMN) 2.0 (2011). http://www.omg.org/spec/BPMN/2.0, Accessed 01 Jun 2016
5. Kossak, F., et al.: A Rigorous Semantics for BPMN 2.0 Process Diagrams. Springer, Cham (2015)
6. Ashby, W.R.: Principles of the self-organizing system. In: Principles of Self-Organization: Transactions of the University of Illinois Symposium, Pergamon, pp. 255–278 (1962)
7. Goldstein, J.: Emergence as a construct: history and issues. Emergence **1**(1), 49–72 (1999)
8. Serugendo, G.D.M., Gleizes, M.P., Karageorgos, A.: Self-organizing system. Self-organising Software. Natural Computing Series, pp. 7–32. Springer, Heidelberg (2011)
9. Richter-von Hagen, C., Ratz, D., Povalej, R.: Towards self-organizing knowledge intensive processes. JUKM **2**, 148–169 (2005)

10. Sungur, C.T., Breitenbücher, U., Leymann, F., Wieland, M.: Context-sensitive adaptive production processes. Procedia CIRP **41**(Complete), 147–152 (2016)
11. Bucchiarone, A., Marconi, A., Pistore, M., Raik, H.: Dynamic adaptation of fragment-based and context-aware business processes. Proc. ICWS **2012**, 33–41 (2012)
12. Pesic, M., Schonenberg, H., van der Aalst, W.M.: Declare: Full support for loosely-structured processes. In: 11th IEEE International Enterprise Distributed Object Computing Conference, EDOC 2007, p. 287. IEEE (2007)
13. Bögl, A., Natschläger, C., Geist, V.: Towards flexibility in business processes by mining process patterns and process instances. Proc. MODELSWARD **2016**, 469–476 (2016)
14. Reijers, H.A., Rigter, J.H.M., van der Aalst, W.M.P.: The case handling case. Int. J. Cooperative Inf. Syst. **12**(3), 365–391 (2003)
15. Börger, E., Stärk, R.: Abstract State Machines: A Method for High-Level System Design and Analysis. Springer, Heidelberg (2003)
16. Kossak, F., Illibauer, C., Geist, V., Natschläger, C., Ziebermayr, T., Freudenthaler, B., Kopetzky, T., Schewe, K.D.: Hagenberg Business Process Modelling Method. Springer, Cham (2016)
17. Natschläger, C., Geist, V.: A layered approach for actor modelling in business processes. Bus. Process Manage. J. **19**, 917–932 (2013)
18. Atlassian: JIRA software. https://www.atlassian.com/software/jira
19. Natschläger, C., Geist, V., Illibauer, C., Hutter, R.: Modelling business process variants using graph transformation rules. Proc. MODELSWARD **2016**, 65–74 (2016)
20. Natschläger, C., Geist, V., Kossak, F., Freudenthaler, B.: Optional activities in process flows. In: Rinderle-Ma, S., Weske, M. (eds.) Proceedings of EMISA 2012 - Der Mensch im Zentrum der Modellierung, Köllen, pp. 67–80 (2012)

Production Processes

Towards Information Management Support in Test and Piloting of Complex Mechatronic Systems: An Industry Case Study

Christian Salomon[1(✉)], Rudolf Ramler[1], Albert Mayrhofer[2], and Gerhard Sperrer[2]

[1] Software Competence Center Hagenberg, Softwarepark 21, 4232 Hagenberg, Austria
{christian.salomon,rudolf.ramler}@scch.at
[2] TRUMPF Maschinen Austria GmbH + Co. KG, Industriepark 24, 4061 Pasching, Austria
{albert.mayrhofer,gerhard.sperrer}@at.trumpf.com

Abstract. Engineering and testing of mechatronic systems is expected to be heavily impacted by Industry 4.0 and big data, which transform the classic hierarchical information model into decentralized, distributed services. However, it is not sufficient to collect and process big volumes of data in order to realize the expected benefits of Industry 4.0. Industry companies have to establish appropriate interfaces and integration strategies with their established engineering processes and the related information systems. In this paper we present our experiences and the enterprise system infrastructure we developed for test and piloting of complex mechatronic systems at a large engineering and manufacturing company. The implemented solution has become a backbone for systems engineering and is frequently used by various stakeholders. Furthermore, we describe how we extend the approach by integrating data from machinery in the field to ensure "end-to-end digital integration" that provides feedback for the construction and testing of new systems.

Keywords: Industry 4.0 · Information integration · Architecture of ERP systems

1 Introduction

The engineering and testing of mechatronic systems is a knowledge-, time- and resource-intensive process. At its core, it is driven by the technical processes of systems engineering [1]. The engineering activities are accompanied by several enterprise and management processes due to their size and organizational complexity. These processes are also the gateway to general business management as well as organizational units that cooperate in the development, deployment, operation and maintenance of the engineered system.

On the enterprise level, processes rely on adequate software support in terms of product lifecycle management tools, manufacturing execution systems and enterprise resource planning (ERP) solutions for implementing business processes, information flows, data visualization and analysis [2]. These software systems are the digital representation of the organizational structures and processes. The classic example in context of production organizations is the archetypal "automation pyramid" [3]. Enterprise

© Springer International Publishing AG 2017
F. Piazolo et al. (Eds.): ERP Future 2016, LNBIP 285, pp. 69–76, 2017.
DOI: 10.1007/978-3-319-58801-8_6

resource planning systems constitute the top level of the pyramid. The base layer is formed by the technical production processes. Vertical integration enables an effective and efficient orchestration of the processes and a timely, data-driven synchronization of the involved activities. The pyramid proposes a hierarchically structured information model where data from different operational processes is integrated and aggregated.

The strategic initiative "Industry 4.0" ("fourth industrial revolution") announced in Germany and its adjunct concepts (e.g., Cloud Computing, Cyber-Physical Systems, Internet of Things) are expected to cause a paradigm shift in work organization, business models and production technology [4]: *"The goal is to realize smart factories, in which machines and resources communicate as in a social network. Such a smart factory will produce intelligent products (smart products) that know how they have been produced, and will collect and transmit data as they are being used; these huge amounts of data (big data) will be collected and analyzed in real time. New insights will thus be generated and used to move one level up from smart factories to smart processes and smart products. At a higher level, the data sent by the smart devices can help the manufacturer to pinpoint the preferences of the consumers and, thus, shape future products"* [5].

Industry 4.0 is also expected to heavily impact the classic hierarchical information model, decomposing the automation pyramid into decentralized, distributed services [6]. Big data is going to play a key role in the paradigm shift. Yet the primary objective behind the use of big data in industrial applications is still to achieve fault-free products and cost efficient running of the processes [5]. Furthermore, the availability of (big) data covering all phases of the product lifecycle – from development and construction, production, usage and end of life – will also leverage the engineering activities involved in complex systems [7] and product lifecycle management [8]. As a result, Industry 4.0 and big data promise a significant economic opportunity. For manufacturing McKinsey estimates a possible decrease in product development and assembly costs by up to 50% and a reduction of working capital by up to seven percent.

However, it is not sufficient to collect and process big volumes of data in order to realize the expected benefits of Industry 4.0. Industry companies have to establish appropriate interfaces and integration strategies with their established engineering processes and the related information systems. This is considered one of the main challenges in related research. Li et al. [8] point out that *"processing engineering data is more than employing existing data process methods to industry cases. To get the desired results which can serve for design, production, maintenance, and recycle, the data processing has to be combined with engineering and manufacturing laws and knowledge"*. Foidl and Felderer [9] analyzed the impact of Industry 4.0 from the viewpoint of an Austrian electronic manufacturing services company. They identified eight fundamental research challenges including the key question *"How should engineering processes and responsibilities be organized along an end-to-end digital integration of engineering?"*.

In this paper we describe an approach and enterprise system infrastructure developed for test and piloting of complex mechatronic systems at a large engineering and manufacturing company, TRUMPF Maschinen Austria. The implemented workflow, information flow, reporting and data analysis support have become a backbone for systems engineering. Currently, the approach is extended to integrate usage data from machinery in the field. The case illustrates a first step towards an "end-to-end digital integration" [6, 9] that forms a feedback cycle providing usage information from the field for the construction and testing of new systems.

This paper is organized as follows: Sect. 2 describes the industry context and the high-level engineering process for mechatronic systems. Section 3 provides an overview of the test and piloting process and the related software infrastructure. Furthermore, this section also discusses requirements and benefits of collecting and integrating field data from machinery usage together with a preliminary solution concept. The paper concludes with a summary and lessons learned in Sect. 4.

2   Industry Context

The high-technology company TRUMPF provides manufacturing solutions in the fields of machine tools, lasers and electronics. These are used in the manufacturing of the most diverse products, from vehicles, building technology and mobile devices to state-of-the-art power and data storage. The company's core business is in machine tools for flexible sheet metal processing and tube processing. With more than 60 international subsidiaries all around the globe, TRUMPF is one of the world's biggest providers of machine tools.

The focus of the work described in this paper is on a specific engineering phase, namely *Test and Piloting*, within the engineering process of mechatronic systems (on the right-hand side of Fig. 1). This process includes integrating of experiences and feedback from the field leading to new or refined requirements specifications that cause adaptation of existing test scenarios. In the company's organization, the test and piloting activities are structured in a stand-alone test and piloting department with interfaces to the different engineering and development departments, the product lifecycle management, and the quality assurance department.

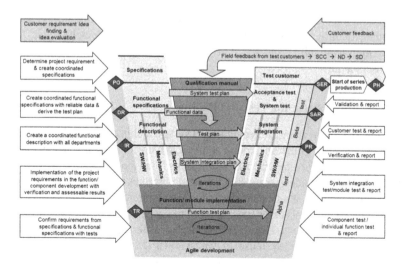

Fig. 1. V-Model as applied in the TRUMPF engineering process

A detailed overview of the workflow is given in [10]. Examples for specific tests are life cycle tests, tests for series-production readiness, accuracy and functional specimen tests. Tests are usually either part of an innovation process or integrated in the development of a new system. Their main purpose lies in the improvement of existing components or in the exploration of the technical capabilities of new components. Reuse of tests and their evolution over product versions and cycles play a central role. Tests for early innovations are transformed into reusable tests that are made available for future test and piloting cycles. As the test and piloting department acts as an internal service department, test and piloting assignments are triggered in all phases of the development process (e.g., concept phase, development phase, prototype phase, prelaunch phase, and series release) and also during the maintenance of production models in case of production series support.

3   System Overview

Test and piloting is a key step in the engineering of new mechatronic systems as it is subject to engineering standards and legal requirements. It is highly data-driven [11] and relies on detailed and accurate documentation of the process and the outcome. The whole process is supported by a custom information system. Since a study conducted with industry partner companies showed that no appropriate support by standard tools or commercial vendors is available [10], a custom solution for test and piloting practices has been developed in-house, enriched with test planning methods, knowledge management for test methods and reuse methods and integrated in the existing infrastructure.

The developed solution, which was built on top of Microsoft Sharepoint, has become a highly successful support system and a valuable backbone for the systems engineering process. It is used throughout the bending technology division of TRUMPF by employees on sites in four different countries (AUT, GER, ITA, and CHN). As a central data hub it does not only serve system engineers and testers but also members of software development, quality assurance, marketing & sales, and product lifecycle support. Therefore, high availability and scalability is a major requirement to serve up to 100 different users a day.

3.1   Information System for Test and Piloting

Figure 2 provides an overview of the high-level system architecture and design of the tool support. Core modules of the Sharepoint solution, which contents are closely coupled to each other, are the *Specification*, the *Test Management*, and the *Test Execution* module. The *Specification* module contains structured data that describes the composition, the context and product line features of a machine as defined in requirements and performance specification documents. On basis of the specifications test and piloting project managers use the Test Management module to create test plans for different project phases. The Test Management module supports reuse of well-known standard tests that were already conducted in similar projects. Furthermore, it provides feedback about the overall testing progress based on information from the Test Execution module.

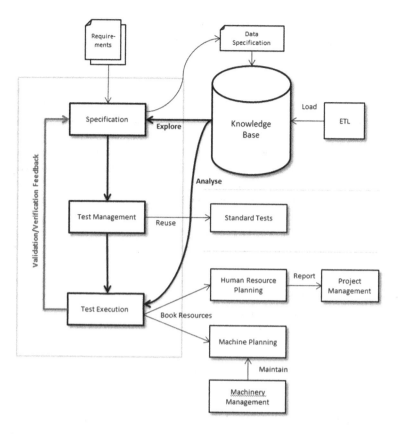

Fig. 2. Overview of the custom tool solution for test and piloting of mechatronic systems.

Items in the *Test Execution* module, so called *test orders*, are generated according to the test plan items. A case offers a detailed description of the testing sequence, helps useres keeping track of their activities, and rates the degree of performance and quality. The ratings of test orders are reported back to the specification module, which provides an overview of the verification and validation state for system engineers. Additionally, the Test Execution module features a fast and easy way to reserve time slots on testing machinery and to assign test execution items to members of the test and piloting depart-ment. By means of this information the project manager is able to monitor the degree of capacity utilization and distribute the workload of testers semi-automatically. Due to the association of test orders with machines it is possible to reproduce the history for traceability reasons.

3.2   Integrating Data from Field Usage

Test and piloting of machines require expert knowledge about typical usage scenarios, exceptional situations and accurate estimates about the frequency of their occurrence in the field. Relevant data is collected in requirements engineering, from previous test and piloting iterations as well as from support and maintenance cases. Currently, the approach is extended to integrate usage data from machinery in the field as a step towards a closed feedback cycle providing most realistic and up-to-date information for the construction and testing of new systems.

For this reason we build up a *Knowledge Base* (Fig. 2) using *Elastic Stack*[1] (including *Logstash*, *Elastic Search*, and *Kibana*). Data in the *Knowledge Base* is constructed from machine logs, which contain information about sequences, parameters, and types of activities. These logs are produced from machinery of different generations and different product lines and, moreover, must be processed from a variety of data sources. Typically the machine logs are not accessible via network but they have to be retrieved from machines in the field by a service technician. An ETL process based on *Logstash* is implemented to harmonize heterogeneous log data and to store them in the knowledge base in a structured way.

Structured data in the *Knowledge Base* may be either manually explored to discover requirements for new usage scenarios or automatically analyzed to support the creation of test cases. Manual exploration – as perfomed by system/mechatronic engineers, sales employees, and product managers – is supported by pre-defined and extensible *Kibana* dashboards. Automatic analyzation is implemented using Elastic Search queries that are framed to serve tools used by simulation engineers [12], software developers, and the present information system for test and piloting.

4   Summary and Lessons Learned

In this paper we described the process and information management infrastructure developed for test and piloting of complex mechatronic systems at TRUMPF Maschinen Austria. The implemented system has become a central data hub for the overall systems engineering process. It is extended to integrate usage data from the field to provide a realistic and accurate basis for constructing and testing of new machinery. In the following we summarize our lessons learned from the development of the information system and its application for an "end-to-end integration" over the entire product life-cycle.

(1) **Developing a custom solution provides optimal support for flexible business processes.** No off-the-shelf solution was available that would have provided the required functionality, which triggered the development of an in-house solution.

Traditional ERP systems unite functions such as order management, procurement, production and inventory management, human resources, as well as financial controlling on a single, integrated platform. Thus, ERP systems have been widely adopted for manufacturing companies. The support has been extended towards capabilities for make-to-order. However, ERP still lacks key functions for systems engineering where the work is often conducted in (one-off) projects not based on orders. Implementing a custom solution turned out to be the right decision, as it offers flexibility and optimal

---

[1] https://www.elastic.co.

adaptation to existing processes and established workflows. These processes and work-flows are core assets of an engineering company. Finally, the custom solution helped to gain high user acceptance.

(2) **A mature web-based technology as platform for the custom solution provides security, accessibility, and scalability.**

Large parts of the system described in this paper were developed on top of Microsoft Sharepoint (see Sect. 3). The main reason for choosing Microsoft Sharepoint as the basis has been its web-based technology that it is accessible to all employees at different sites and via various different (mobile) devices. At the same time it is scalable enough to introduce new projects and services without affecting the performance of the system.

(3) **Early user involvement supported by an incremental development approach is crucial for the acceptance of the system.**

After establishing a data base, features have initially been implemented by rapid prototyping. New features were deployed and released to a set of core users, who provided fast feedback. Features that were used frequently have been improved according to the feedback and brought to product maturity, e.g., by increasing automation support. Features not in use were discarded or replaced by different functionality. This user-centered design approach ensured that features have been implemented properly and it raised acceptance of the whole solution.

(4) **Two distinct scenarios must be supported when integrating machinery data from the field.**

Scenario 1: Users expect the possibility to explore data via dashboards, business intelligence, or data analysis to gain new, "surprising" insights that impact the existing processes and engineering activities in "revolutionary" new ways. For example, creating completely new tests/requirements from previously unknown usage scenarios and design new piloting approaches with real-time feedback from the field.

Scenario 2: The most frequent and therefore essential scenario, however, remains the integration of data as part of established processes and engineering activities, which are not changed radically because of new insights from data. The goal is to support existing processes and activities by easy integration of information, making them more accurate and speeding up testing cycles.

(5) **Management support and the presence of a project champion are critical success factors when implementing an ERP solution.**

Building up an ERP system is a time-intensive process that includes concerns of various different stakeholders. Therefore, one of the most important success factors is top management support [13]. In the present case the manager in charge actively participates and backs up the project even when the project team gets on the wrong track and features have to be discarded.

Furthermore, the *"success of technological innovations has often been linked to the presence of a champion, who performs the crucial functions of transformational leadership, facilitation, and marketing the project to the users"* [14]. The project team contained a member who, on the one hand, took care of entering a critical amount of data in the initialization phase to make sure that colleagues had additional benefits when using the system at an early stage. On the other hand this team member also built up a network of users to gain feedback, requirements and to promote the system.

References

1. Walden, D., Roedler, G.J., Forsberg, K.J., Hamelin, D., Shortell, T.M.: INCOSE Systems Engineering Handbook: A Guide for System Life Cycle Processes and Activities, 4th edn. Wiley (2015)
2. Jessup, L.M., Valacich, J.S.: Information Systems Today: Managing in the Digital World. Pearson Prentice Hall, Upper Saddle River (2008)
3. Vogel-Heuser, B., Kegel, G., Bender, K., Wucherer, K.: Global information architecture for industrial automation. Automatisierungstechnische Praxis (atp) **51**(1), 108–115 (2009)
4. Bauernhansl, T., Ten Hompel, M., Vogel-Heuser, B. (eds.): Industrie 4.0 in Produktion, Automatisierung und Logistik: Anwendung, Technologien, Migration. Springer (2014)
5. Yin, S., Kaynak, O.: Big Data for Modern Industry: Challenges and Trends. Proc. IEEE **103**(2), 143–146 (2015)
6. Monostori, L.: Cyber-physical production systems: roots, expectations and R&D challenges. In: Proceedings of the 47th CIRP Conference on Manufacturing Systems 17, pp. 9–13 (2014)
7. Pang, C.K., Ng, T.S., Lewis, F.L., Lee, T.H.: Managing complex mechatronics R&D: a systems design approach. IEEE Trans. Syst. Man, Cybern. Part A: Syst. Humans **42**(1), 57–67 (2012)
8. Li, J., Tao, F., Cheng, Y., Zhao, L.: Big Data in product lifecycle management. Int. J. Adv. Manuf. Technol. **81**(1–4), 667–684 (2015)
9. Foidl, H., Felderer, M.: Research challenges of industry 4.0 for quality management. In: Felderer, M., Piazolo, F., Ortner, W., Brehm, L., Hof, H.-J. (eds.) ERP 2015. LNBIP, vol. 245, pp. 121–137. Springer, Cham (2016). doi:10.1007/978-3-319-32799-0_10
10. Zeilinger, R., Beer, W., Mayrhofer, A., Wesinger, M.: A survey on test and piloting practices within the engineering of industrial machines and facilities. In: IEEE International Conference on Emerging Technology and Factory Automation (ETFA), Barcelona (2014)
11. Armes, T., Refern, M.: Using Big Data and predictive machine learning in aerospace test environments. In: IEEE AUTOTESTCON (2013)
12. Friedl, M., Scheidl, R., Hehenberger, P., Kellner, A., Weingartner, L., Hörl, M.: A design optimization framework for multidisciplinary mechatronic systems. In: Proceedings of TMCE 2016 - Tools and Methods for Competitive Engineering, pp. 3–12 (2016)
13. Somers, T.M., Nelson, K.: The impact of critical success factors across the stages of enterprise resource planning implementations. In: Proceedings of the 34th Annual Hawaii International Conference on System Sciences, p. 10 (2001)
14. Akkermans, H., van Helden, K.: Vicious and virtuous cycles in ERP implementation: a case study of interrelations between critical success factors. Eur. J. Inf. Syst. **11**(1), 35–46 (2002)

Security Aspects and Models in Cooperative Production Processes

Dagmar Auer[1(✉)] and Josef Küng[2]

[1] Institute for Application Oriented Knowledge Processing (FAW),
Johannes Kepler University Linz (JKU),
Softwarepark 35, 4232 Hagenberg im Mühlkreis, Austria
dagmar.auer@jku.at
[2] Institute for Application Oriented Knowledge Processing (FAW),
Johannes Kepler University Linz (JKU), Altenbergerstr. 69, 4040 Linz, Austria
josef.kueng@jku.at

Abstract. Cooperative production is increasingly important in today's globalized competitive economy, especially for small and medium-sized enterprises
(SME). Companies work together and by this share their competencies, information and resources to optimize production. The flexibility demands towards
the supporting software applications not only concern the processes and services,
but also security aspects. In this paper we focus on access control. A range of
security models is studied with respect to their suitability of fulfilling the security
requirements for cooperative production. Included are established models such
as role-based access control (RBAC), or noticeable ones like attribute-based
access control (ABAC), but also rather little-known ones such as break-the-glass
(BTG) or intend-based access control (IBAC). The requirements discussed are
based on literature study and results of a current application-oriented research
project. Finally a recommendation for some specific security models is argued.

Keywords: Cooperative production · Cooperative production processes ·
Security · Security requirements · Security models

1 Introduction

In today's globalized competitive economy the need for well-organized cooperative
production networks is increasing continuously, especially for small and medium-sized
enterprises (SME). With this business paradigm, individual companies work together
and share their competencies to optimize production and the own results.

Cooperating is not a completely new approach, but often, especially with SMEs,
companies still work together on a rather informal basis - they know each other, they
trust each other and thus, when needed they contact each other to join a cooperative job.
There is little or no specific IT support. It is rather about phone calls and e-mails send
around.

A cooperative production network is much more than that. Different partners work
together in not only one but several projects – be it in parallel or in sequence. The network

© Springer International Publishing AG 2017
F. Piazolo et al. (Eds.): ERP Future 2016, LNBIP 285, pp. 77–86, 2017.
DOI: 10.1007/978-3-319-58801-8_7

is based on a common strategy, the members share their knowledge and experience in a much broader way than before, several partners may be involved in one job, and many more aspects. Cooperative jobs are characterized by a high need of flexibility, contractual relations with quite a number of partners, instantly reacting to internal and external events, adding new partners and/or removing ones, generally leaving planning details open until they are actually needed, etc. Such a network is typically supported by some specific software tool. Besides the services offered, it is always a question about security, especially access rights. Even though trust is said to be a fundamental basis for such a cooperative production network, the level of trust may not be the same between each of the partners. Thus, challenging security requirements, especially concerning access rights need to be considered in the software system. Therefore, an appropriate security model needs to be selected to support these requirements. How fit models such discretionary access control (DAC), mandatory access control (MAC, lattice based access control) or role-based access control (RBAC) the requirements? What about attribute-based access control (ABAC), the Chinese wall security models, Break-the-Glass (BTG), Intend-based Access Control (IBAC) or Emotion-based Access Control (EBAC)?

In the further this paper discusses different security models with respect to the specific security requirements of cooperative production processes. The paper is structured as follows: Section 2 starts with a discussion of the terms cooperation vs. collaboration, which are often used interchangeably, not only in practice. In the further, basic ideas concerning cooperative production in small and medium-sized enterprises (SME) and cooperation networks are discussed. In the following Sect. 3 essential security requirements for cooperative production processes, considering theory but also experiences from a current application-oriented research project, are given. Several possibly useful alternative security models are discussed in Sect. 4 with respect to the security requirements described before, to propose a suitable security concept concerning access control for cooperative production processes in SMEs. The conclusion in Sect. 5 finally rounds up the paper.

2   Cooperative Production in SMEs

Tough competition in today's globalized economy demands companies, especially small and medium-sized enterprises (SME), to cooperate to survive on the market [1]. Cooperative production is a business paradigm, where individual companies work together and share their competencies to optimize production within the network [2] and reinforce each other.

Especially in practice the two manifestations of working together – cooperation and collaboration – are often used interchangeable. Research and professional literature attempt to overcome this shortcoming by providing definitions, but still they are not used consistently also in literature.

After [3] the term *cooperation* implies a varying degree of intensity, duration and direction of cooperation between independent companies. The partners can be both competitors, as well as upstream or downstream in the value chain. In scientific work the following characteristics have be derived:

- A common goal or activity is split into differently weighted sub-tasks (*division of labor*), which can be processed sequentially or in parallel (see [4, 5]).
- The cooperation is organized through a *hierarchical structure* (dictate, subordination, different duties) [4, 5].
- The partners are *legally and partially economically independent* [6, 7].
- Often considered, but not regarded as essential aspects are: the use of *common resources* for the individual preparation of the results [5] as well as a *cooperation agreement* [6]. [5, p 37] summarizes cooperation briefly as "activity and process coordination".

In the professional world *collaboration* is often seen as a stronger form of cooperation. [4] differentiates the terms cooperation and collaboration in particular with regard to the type of division of labor. While work is centrally allocated in a cooperation, in a collaboration each contributes "… alike with his individual knowledge and skills for solving the overall task …".

The following characteristics are often associated with collaboration:

- Individuals, groups, organizations, etc. *jointly work at the same time* on a common goal or task [4–6].
- *Context* is *designed and negotiated together* [6].
- *Ongoing decentralized decisions* within common process chains, who makes a certain contribution [4].
- The *individual contribution* to the overall result is *not always accurately traceable* [4], as they are not only directly measurable, but also influence each other [6].
- *Shared resources* and *distributed information* [5].

Even though in practice many production steps are often rather executed in cooperation, there are crucial parts which need collaboration, too. Collaboration between companies differs from approaches such as computer-supported collaborative work (CSCW) which denotes a class of software applications, supporting people to cooperate within an organization (cp. [8]). As the focus with our project is on the characteristics stated with cooperation, we will further keep with this term.

Cooperative production is about achieving individual and common goals, by streamlining and coordinating the whole production and service process, including the supply chain. With current IT infrastructures this also means to provide interfaces or some common space to allow for a comprehensive and coherent common information base, which is important to support and improve decision taking throughout the whole process.

However, there is not the one cooperation model. Cooperation can differ in many aspects, be it in type (production, production creation, research, joint venture, etc.) or scope (single interaction, long-lasting cooperation with several partners). [7] for example differentiates cooperation types based on their primary goals – interest group/syndicate, consortium, and joint venture. While a *syndicate* strives for long-term profit maximization by merging purchasing, marketing and sales or product development, a *consortium* works together on a certain task or goal, e.g., constructing a complete building. A *joint venture* means jointly establishing a legally independent company that performs tasks in the common interest. But there are many other types of cooperation models. The design heavily depends on the framework conditions, the partners involved – their strategies, needs and competencies – and particularly the trust that they have in each other. Thus, different contractual relations need to be defined with each cooperative job, with details depending on the set of partners involved (cp. [9]).

Not only with collaboration, but also with cooperation organizations need to adjust their strategies and especially their operative processes throughout the whole value-chain to successfully work together (cp. [2]). The need to negotiate the concrete layout of the cooperation could be supported by methods used with e-Contracting based on semantic technologies. [10] demonstrate a modular framework using Semantic Web technologies for e-Contracting, where communication protocols and the strategies of all partners involved are separated to enhance reusability and offer better support for privacy and security issues.

2.1 Dynamic Manufacturing Networks

During the last years the term *Dynamic Manufacturing Network* (*DMN*) has emerged, meaning permanent or temporarily production cooperation between SMEs, which work together in a common value chain to achieve better results. The intention behind the development of the term DMN was to increase competitiveness through a stronger focus on core competencies and partnerships with other organizations with complementary strengths [11, 12].

The term DMN was introduced in [13] and further developed in the European project *IMAGINE* [11], where the cooperation platform *i-platform* has been developed to implement and support DMNs. A DMN can be regarded as production or supply chain network, with an implicit concept of dynamics to react to changing market demands. The project IMAGINE had a strong focus on dynamic partner selection, which is however not the core problem in our scenarios, but still the basic framework developed throughout IMAGINE is an interesting starting point for our project.

To participate in a DMN needs to be a well-considered decision at each participating organization. Many things need to be regarded such as trust, security, need for adopting internal processes and IT interfaces to correspond to certain DMN-specific standards, resistance against change (esp. in the initial phase), but also loss in money and reputation if the network fails. But on the other hand, studies prove that DMNs, if well-functioning, generate profit already in the initial phase up to 30% [14] by decreasing management and production costs and reducing quality problems at the same time. Additional advantages are furthermore the reduced financial commitment of the partners and much better times to market [15, 16].

In the project IMAGINE a DMN lifecycle model has been developed which describes three phases: (1) Networks Analysis & Configuration, (2) Network Design, and (3) Network Execution Management & Monitoring [17] (Fig. 1).

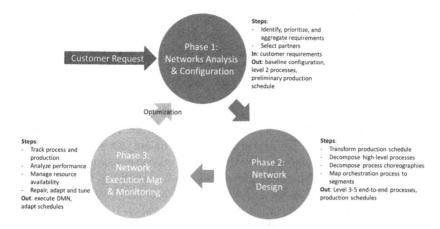

Fig. 1. DMN lifecycle model [17]

The cycle starts with a customer request, describing the requirements for a certain order (e.g., kind of product including details, delivery date). In phase 1 the consortium is created, which consists of production partners and suppliers. Furthermore, all necessary information is prepared. During phase 2 all processes are setup in the network (end-to-end), while phase 3 deals with the execution of these processes and their controlling within the network. The focus of the IMAGINE project is on each cooperative job.

2.2 Dynamic Enterprise Network

While the focus of IMAGINE is on the DMN lifecycle of each single cooperation, [18] further distinguishes between the underlying stable corporate network and the dynamic, job-oriented value added network (see Fig. 2). The value added network, called the Virtual Enterprise, is built upon a stable platform, which covers all partners that handle common jobs under this network. The platform describes the roles that the partners can

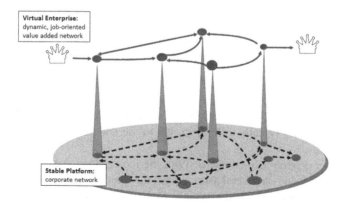

Fig. 2. Virtual Enterprise and Stable Platform (cp. [18, p. 323])

take over regarding the development of the network itself, but also in terms of concrete cooperative jobs.

Technical interfaces between the partners are defined, to facilitate an integrated IT support. In addition, a variety of information is documented in this platform, such as contact lists, special partners' skills or experience, suppliers, history of cooperative jobs, or basic contractual arrangements.

The corporate network can be designed to be very open right up to be completely isolated. The design is driven by the strategy for the network. However, studies have shown [18] that completely open networks in practice do not survive in the long term. A core team that strongly identifies itself with the network and is working on a consistent goal-oriented development is essential for the successful viability of the network.

Based on this network, job-based, dynamic value chains can be defined in different compositions. Not each partner participates in each job, and also the responsibilities of a partner can change from job to job. Depending on the requirements, the consortium is formed and may even been further developed throughout the job.

The dynamics implied in the basic concept, but also the need to support some common ground, have to be considered with the supporting IT infrastructure.

3   Security Requirements for Cooperative Production Processes

Even though security requirements are not only relevant within the context of one specific application, we will concentrate on the requirements concerning the information system implementing the processes. Cooperative production processes involve several partners in distinct locations. Thus, communication between these partners is transmitted over some network, typically the Internet. Therefore communication over the network as well as the IT system needs to be protected.

In the further, we focus on the security requirements for the cooperative production processes, especially on access rights. Besides theoretical considerations, the following requirements are based on results from one of our current application-oriented research projects, dealing with cooperative production processes. We only point out the most important requirements:

- *Different levels of stability of access rights.* Cooperation processes are characterized by a high demand for flexibility, which needs to be considered with the security requirements for the supporting IT system. As proposed by [18], we distinguish between the stable platform and the job-oriented network. The stable platform holds general information about the partners, interfaces, etc., and needs rather stable access rights to the different artifacts in the IT system. The job-oriented network, however, supports the individual, dynamically evolving cooperative job. For these cooperative jobs, access rights typically differ from job to job and may also change during its development.
- *Flexibility in defining access rights.* With the job-oriented networks, the concrete access rights depend on several aspects from the basic characteristics of the cooperation type, to the customer and especially to the other partners involved. There may be different levels of trust between the partners involved within the network, which

needs to be taken into account. E.g., while some partner would not care sharing detailed data with partner A, it would be absolutely impossible with partner B. For successfully establishing cooperative production processes also such special cases need to be considered.

- *Management of access rights within the job-oriented network.* This requirement is based on the high demand for flexibility. The detailed definition of access rights for the concrete job should be managed by the one responsible for the concrete job. As flexibility in processes is managed by this person, this is also the one who best knows about the specific security demands within the specific situation and can continuously keep processes and security aligned.
- *Immediate changes.* Changes to security-relevant aspects need to be immediately available within the information system. Cooperative jobs are continuously evolving in a typically stressful time frame, therefore new team members need to be integrated quickly, changes to access rights of different artifacts need to be directly available, etc.
- *Immediate reaction in urgency.* Even though the domain is not dealing with life-threatening processes, still in some situations (e.g., disease, offense, accident, or death) immediate reaction can be crucial for the economic survival of partners. Especially, if the individual processes are very much integrated with the ones of the other partners. Yes, production networks are one mean to distribute risk, but they are also established to go for larger projects. Immediate reaction may leverage the existing access rules, but still may be necessary, at least for active users within the system, perhaps with additional limitations. If so, mechanisms for monitoring what happened then, being able to roll up the whole case are necessary.

The security models studied in the following will then be analyzed concerning the high-level requirements presented before.

4   Security Models for Cooperative Production Processes in SMEs

There are three models that are mostly used in practice for securing information in terms of access control, *discretionary access control (DAC)* [19], *mandatory access control (MAC,* lattice-based access control) [20] and *role-based access control (RBAC)* [21, 22]. Out of them RBAC has become the dominant model. Quite some extensions of RBAC have been developed like introducing hierarchies [21] or adding spatial concepts (SRBAC) [23].

Anyhow another approach came up, defining access via attributes. It allows much more flexibility and helps to overcome the strict subject – object – access right restrictions. The *attribute-based access control (ABAC)* has been developed and proposed by [24]. Due to its flexibility the other models (DAC, MAC, RBAC) can be defined in ABAC [25]. Frameworks and standards like the OASIS XACML (eXtensible Access Control Markup Language) have been developed and are used in practice, mainly supporting this new ABAC model.

For separating information access between different companies the *Chinese wall security model* was developed. The main idea is that first users are able to access any information from any company but, once one has accessed data from one company, he or she is no longer allowed to access information from another company within the same class of companies. So no information flow can happen between two competing companies. According to the authors this model is also known as *Brewer and Nash Model* [26].

Beyond this 'classics' lots of other not so well known security models have been introduced. Three of them shall be listed here. First we have to mention the *'Break the Glass' model* (*BTG*). It mainly has its origin in the medical domain [27]. Solutions to access the medical data of a patient, although prohibited by the access control system, are required in case of an emergency. Basically the main idea is that the system allows breaking access restrictions defined in a chosen other security model, e.g., RBAC. In such a case predefined actions are performed, e.g., protocolling everything in detail and immediately informing authorities about this event. A simple implementation would to prepare particular user-accounts for such situations and to start according measures automatically when one of these accounts is used. Newer research also incorporates break-glass-policies into other domains, such as business processes. A sound review has been published in [28].

All models listed above ask "who" (verified by an authentication procedure) wants access and then according to the model specific regulations allow or deny it. A completely different approach to access control is asking "why" access is wanted. These models are called *Intend-based Access Control* (*IBAC*) or *Emotion-based Access Control* (*EBAC*). The big - in our view still open - research question is how to detect intention and emotion correctly. The first publications are doing it by measuring and classifying EEG signals from the users' brains [29] which currently is no option in daily practice.

Matching the requirements described in Sect. 3 with the security models available we can argue:

- MAC, DAC, RBAC (the most popular models) do not support sufficiently the required flexibility.
- Chinese wall could be an approach, but seems not to be the right one for these particular application scenarios. E.g., it does not allow that one partner will get information from a second partner in the same group. Through the dynamics the groups would have to be reassigned very often.
- ABAC definitely is a candidate. Access right rules can be defined completely free (E.g., like "If the owner of the data belongs to the same project then allow access.") However, defining and managing all of these partly fine-grained rules causes additional effort and has to be supported very well.
- IBAC and EBAC are by far too futuristic and will not be candidates for cooperative production in SMEs.
- We propose the combination of BTG and ABAC to be the best combination of models. Here we have the flexibility of ABAC but it can be applied in a compact way. Not each situation or eventuality must be considered. For these cases BTG will step into and guarantee the right information flows.

The results given provide some basic orientation for the decision concerning an appropriate model or model-mix. Besides this, additional criteria have to be regarded in a concrete situation, especially with respect to the competences of the users involved.

5 Conclusion

Beside economic aspects like optimizing resources and gaining a better profit in loosely coupled production networks security aspects are important as well. In this article well known but also some not so widespread approaches for security models and policies are investigated towards their applicability for production networks. The attribute-based access control definitively fits the requirements of cooperative production in SMEs best, since it allows a completely free definition of access rules. Managing the access rules will take some effort and resources. Here adding a break-the-glass implementation could help. On one hand it allows to implement a more restrictive policy without the need of frequent changes, on the other hand it will allow to continue a process, even if the according access rules do not allow it – of course with a detailed documentation and information chain of this event.

References

1. Firmansyah, M.R., Amer, Y.: A review of collaborative manufacturing network models. Int. J. Mater. Mech. Manufact. **1**(1), 6–12 (2013)
2. McClellan, M.: Collaborative manufacturing: a strategy built on trust and cooperation. Control Solution Int. **12**, 27–31 (2003)
3. Gabler Wirtschaftslexikon, Springer Gabler. http://wirtschaftslexikon.gabler.de
4. Schmalz, S.: Zwischen Kooperation und Kollaboration, zwischen Hierarchie und Heterarchie. Organisationsprinzipien und -strukturen von Wikis. In: Stegbauer, C., Schmidt, J., Schönberger, K. (Hrsg.): Wikis: Diskurse, Theorien und Anwendungen. Sonderausgabe von kommunikation@gesellschaft, Jg. 8. Online-Publikation (2007). http://www.soz.uni-frankfurt.de/K.G/B5_2007_Schmalz.pdf
5. Stoller-Schai, D.: E-Collaboration: Die Gestaltung internetgestützter kollaborativer Handlungsfelder. Dissertation, Universität St. Gallen; Hochschule für Wirtschafts- Rechts- und Sozialwissenschaften (HSG) (2003)
6. Etter, C.: Nachgründungsdynamik neugegründeter Unternehmen in Berlin im interregionalen Vergleich. Dissertation, FU Berlin (2003)
7. Killich S.: Aufbau erfolgreicher Unternehmenskooperationen – Ein Leitfaden für mittelständische Automobilzulieferer. Luczak, H. (Hrsg.), Forschungsinstitut für Rationalisierung, Lehrstuhl und Institut Arbeitswissenschaften (FIR + IAW), RWTH Aachen, Sonderdruck 06/00, 1. Auflage, Aachen (2000)
8. Draheim, D.: Smart business process management. In: Fischer, L. (ed.) Social BPM: work, planning and collaboration under the impact of social technology. BPM and workflow handbook series, digital edn. Future Strategies Inc., Lighthouse Point (2011)
9. Jensen, M.C., Meckling, W.H.: Theory of the firm: managerial behavior, agency costs and ownership structure. SSRN J. (1998)
10. Kravari, K., Papavasileiou, C., Bassiliades, N.: Knowledge-based e-contract negotiation among agents using semantic web technologies. In: Bădică, C., Nguyen, N.T., Brezovan, M. (eds.) ICCCI 2013. LNCS, vol. 8083, pp. 215–224. Springer, Heidelberg (2013). doi:10.1007/978-3-642-40495-5_22
11. Ferreira, J., Gigante, F., Sarraipa, J., Nunez, M.J., Agostinho, C., Jardim-Goncalves, R.: Collaborative production using dynamic manufacturing networks for SME's. In: International ICE Conference on Engineering, Technology and Innovation (ICE), pp. 1–7 (2014)

12. Papakostas, N., Efthymiou, K., Georgoulias, K., Chryssolouris, G.: On the configuration and planning of dynamic manufacturing networks. Logistics Res. **5**(3–4), 105–111 (2012)
13. Viswanadham, N., Gaonkar, R.S.: Partner selection and synchronized planning in dynamic manufacturing networks. IEEE Trans. Robot. Autom. **19**(1), 117–130 (2003)
14. Chalmeta, R., Grangel, R.: Performance measurement systems for virtual enterprise integration. Int. J. Comput. Integr. Manuf. **18**(1), 73–84 (2005)
15. Renton, W.J., Rudnick, F.C., Brown, R.G.: Virtual manufacturing technology implementation at boeing. In: Proceeding 85th AGARD SMP Meeting on Virtual Manufacturing, Aalborg (1997)
16. Santoro, R., Conte, M.: Evaluation of benefits and advantages of the virtual enterprise approach adoption for actual business cases. In: Proceeding 8th International Conference on Concurrent Enterprising (2002)
17. Markaki, O., Panopoulos, D., Kokkinakos, P., Koussouris, S., Askounis, D.: Towards adopting dynamic manufacturing networks for future manufacturing: benefits and risks of the IMAGINE DMN end-to-end management methodology. In: 22nd International Workshop on Enabling Technologies: Infrastructure for Collaborative Enterprises (WETICE), pp. 305–310. IEEE (2013)
18. Schuh, G., Sauer, A., Schönung, M.: Management von Unternehmensnetzwerken – Konzepte zur Gestaltung, Lenkung und Entwicklung. In: Bullinger, H.-J., Spath, D., Warnecke, H.-J., Westkämper, E. (eds.) Handbuch Unternehmensorganisation – Strategien, Planung, Umsetzung, 3rd edn, pp. 318–332. Springer, Berlin Heidelberg (2009)
19. Sandhu, R.S., Samarati, P.: Access control: principles and practice. IEEE Commun. Mag. **32**(9), 40–48 (1994)
20. Sandhu, R.S.: Lattice-based access control models. In: IEEE Computer (1993)
21. Sandhu, R.S., Coyne, E.J., Feinstein, H.L., Youman, C.E.: Role-based access control models. In: IEEE Computer, pp. 38–47. IEEE Press (1996)
22. Ferraiolo, D.F., Sandhu, R.S., Gavrila, S., Kuhn, D.R., Chandramouli, R.: Proposed NIST standard for role-based access control. ACM Trans. Inf. Syst. Secur. **4**(3), 224–274 (2001)
23. Hansen, F., Oleshchuk, V.: SRBAC: a spatial role-based access control model for mobile systems. In: Proceedings of the Seventh Nordic Workshop on Secure IT Systems (Nordsec 2003), 15–17 October, pp. 129–141 (2003)
24. Hu, V.C., Ferraiolo, D., Kuhn, R., Schnitzer, A., Sandlin, K., Miller, R., Scarfone K.: Guide to Attribute Based Access Control (ABAC) Definition and Considerations. NIST Special Publication 800-162, National Institute of Standards and Technology (2014)
25. Jin, X., Krishnan, R., Sandhu, R.: A unified attribute-based access control model covering DAC, MAC and RBAC. In: Cuppens-Boulahia, N., Cuppens, F., GarciaAlfaro, J. (eds.) DBSec 2012, LNCS, vol. 7371, pp. 41–55. Springer, Heidelberg (2012)
26. Brewer, D., Nash, M.: The chinese wall security policy. In: Proceeding 10th IEEE Symposium on Security and Privacy, pp. 206–214 (1989)
27. Break-glass: An approach to granting emergency access to healthcare systems. White Paper, Joint NEMA/COCIR/JIRA Security and Privacy Committee (SPC) (2004)
28. Schefer-Wenzl, S., Bukvova, H., Strembeck, M.: A review of delegation and break-glass models for flexible access control management. In: Abramowicz, W., Kokkinaki, A. (eds.) BIS 2014. LNBIP, vol. 183, pp. 93–104. Springer, Cham (2014). doi:10.1007/978-3-319-11460-6_9
29. Almehmadi, A., El-Khatib, K.: On the possibility of insider threat prevention using Intent-Based Access Control (IBAC). IEEE Syst. J. **99**, 1–12 (2015)

A Practical Approach for Process Mining in Production Processes

Christine Natschläger[✉], Felix Kossak, Christian Lettner, Verena Geist,
Andreas Denkmayr, and Beate Käferböck

Software Competence Center Hagenberg GmbH, Hagenberg, Austria
{christine.natschlager,felix.kossak,christian.lettner,
verena.geist,andreas.denkmayr,beate.kaferbock}@scch.at
https://www.scch.at

Abstract. Processes are the core of an enterprise and describe the interconnection of tasks in daily business. The purpose of this article is to present methods and tools that enable extraction of processes based on the concept of process analysis/mining. This valuable knowledge about the current processes of a company can serve as the starting point for performance analysis and process improvement, for implementation of a software system or for monitoring adherence to processes.

In this paper, we present two actual business scenarios of manufacturing companies and their requirements regarding process analysis. We used a practical research approach including quantitative methods. Important results are the suggestion of a procedure and the development of a process mining tool. A comparison of *de jure* and *de facto* processes and a suggestion of optimization potentials complete the work.

Keywords: Process mining · Process comparison · Optimization

1 Introduction

In administration and semi-automatic production, data is produced in many different places. Analysis of these data is, if at all, mostly done selectively for a specific machine and, thus, represents the view of this machine. To also receive the view of a product, data must be exploited across all production and administrative steps. Process analysis (or process mining) considers the entire process with all its steps and, thus, identifies possible orders of activity execution, misbehavior, outliers, bottlenecks and execution/waiting times.

Process mining is, however, a rather new technology, e.g., in contrast to data mining. According to Gartner's Hype Cycle for Business Process Management,

The research reported in this paper has been supported by the Austrian Ministry for Transport, Innovation and Technology, the Federal Ministry of Science, Research and Economy, and the Province of Upper Austria in the frame of the COMET center SCCH. This publication has been written within the project *AdaBPM* (number 842437), which is funded by the *Austrian Research Promotion Agency* (FFG).

F. Piazolo et al. (Eds.): ERP Future 2016, LNBIP 285, pp. 87–95, 2017.
DOI: 10.1007/978-3-319-58801-8_8

automated business process discovery is currently at the peak of inflated expectations and will reach productivity in about five years [1]. The Process Mining Manifesto [2], which contains a set of guiding principles and was written by the IEEE Task Force on Process Mining, was announced in 2011 and also the well-known book on *Process Mining* by van der Aalst was published in the same year [3]. Thus, the application of process mining techniques in production companies is at an early stage. To address this issue, we provide a practical approach with understandable analysis techniques for typical production processes.

The remainder of this paper is structured as follows: Sect. 2 comprises the motivation and preliminaries of process mining. Related work with focus on process analysis and process mining tools is studied in Sect. 3. In Sect. 4, two business scenarios with production processes are presented and a self-developed process mining tool called "SCCH Process AnT" is described in Sect. 5. Finally, the conclusion sums up the main results in Sect. 6.

2   Motivation and Preliminaries

The aim of process mining is to identify processes from company and/or production data. This includes the identification of activities (process steps), the order and frequency of their execution, as well as the determination of execution-/waiting-/cycle-times. An example for the result of a process analysis is shown in Fig. 1(a). The activities are denoted with capital letters (A, B, C, ...) and comprise the execution time in a confidence interval. The paths between the activities represent the execution order and further specify the absolute and relative frequency as well as the waiting time in a confidence interval. This abstract representation is only one possibility of a process analysis visualization, but it was used as basis for the "SCCH Process AnT" tool (see, e.g., Fig. 1(b)).

The resulting process model is called *de facto* (or *is*) process model, since it pictures the real process execution. This is also the main difference between process mining and classical business process management (BPM). BPM is based on a top-down approach, i.e. a process model is defined (also called *de jure* or *should* process model) and then this process is implemented by IT and executed in the production process. However, deviations may occur in practical execution, thus, compliance cannot be guaranteed. In contrast, process mining provides a bottom-up approach. It is based on the executed production process, identifies the corresponding data and creates a fitting process model (*de facto* process model) with detailed information about execution paths and frequencies. In an optimal case, both, the *de jure* and *de facto* process models, are available, so that discrepancies can be identified by a conformance check.

The resulting *de facto* process model allows to discover bottlenecks, identify outliers and misbehavior, recognize patterns and to prevent process abortion. A detailed performance analysis will further identify optimization potentials and improve, e.g., execution order and execution-/waiting-times. Further potentials of process mining are process monitoring (regular analysis) as well as process simulation and prediction. Challenges in process mining are different data sources

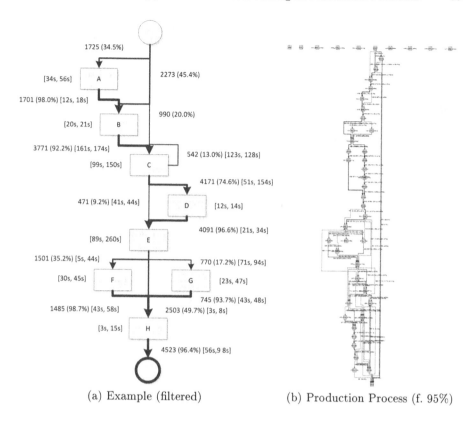

(a) Example (filtered)   (b) Production Process (f. 95%)

Fig. 1. Process analysis

(due to different administration systems and production machines), identification and correction of incomplete and incorrect data, selection of fitting mining algorithms as well as process changes (concept drifts).

3   Related Work

Mining business processes has become a major field of interest in recent years. In particular, existing work on process mining focuses on reconstructing meaningful process models from process instances [3–5]. In that context, a process instance is considered as a sequence of steps captured by process execution logs produced by some process aware information systems. Given a process execution log, the goal is to discover a *de facto* process model, which is capable of explaining exactly all the episodes in the process execution log. Main characteristics of process mining are that (i) it is not limited to control-flow discovery (also considers process conformance and enhancement as well as organizational and time perspective), (ii) it is not a specific type of data mining (new types of representations and algorithms are needed) and (iii) process analysis is not limited to post-mortem analysis (process simulation and prediction) [2].

In previous research, we provided a formal representation of the syntactical definitions of the *Business Process Model and Notation* (BPMN) within an ontology called the BPMN 2.0 Ontology [6] and defined the semantics of BPMN based on Abstract State Machines (ASMs) [7]. We then suggested several extensions addressing inconsistencies and incompleteness and called it the *Hagenberg Business Process Modelling Method* (H-BPM) [8]. We further applied process mining in an approach for flexible business processes to mine process patterns and offer them as alternatives at run-time [9,10].

Several concepts and technologies are related to process mining. For example, *business process intelligence* is a general concept referring to the application of business intelligence techniques to business processes. It comprises a large range of application areas spanning from process discovery to process monitoring, conformance checking, prediction and optimization [11]. *Business activity monitoring* refers to the analysis and presentation of real-time information about activities from multiple application systems [12]. *Data analysis/mining* [13] investigates data to discover patterns using methods like statistical, machine learning and neural networks. Furthermore, *decision mining* aims at the detection of data dependencies that affect the routing of cases and may be used within process mining [14].

Process mining (or a technical process analysis) must, however, be distinguished from well-known *economical process analysis* [15]. The goal of an economical process analysis is to identify the process and its steps based on investigation, questionnaires and interviews. Hence, it considers the knowledge of experts already at a very early stage. However, the received process will be inaccurate and vague, since nobody can exactly say, how often which production path was taken, how often misbehavior occurred or what the exact execution time was for thousands of produced items. In contrast, a *technical process analysis* identifies detailed data already at the beginning and includes expert knowledge later when optimizing the process. It is, however, a good idea to combine technical and economical process analysis to provide a comprehensive process description.

Several process mining tools support a technical process analysis. For example, the process mining tool *ProM* is an open-source framework, mainly used for academic research in the scientific community [3,5]. It provides about 300 plug-ins for mining, analysis, import, export, conversion and filtering. We used *ProM* to analyze the log files of our business cases but encountered problems regarding stability, representation of outliers and data limits (log files had to be partitioned). The commercial spin-off of *ProM* is the widely used process mining tool *Disco* of the company *Fluxicon*. This tool provides automated process discovery, process map animation, statistics and filtering techniques. Another commercial tool in the German-speaking region is *Celonis Process Mining*, which provides a dashboard as well as process discovery with statistics and identification of process variants. There are several further process mining tools like, e.g., *QPR Process Analyzer*, *SNP Business Process Analysis*, *Perceptive Process Mining*, *Rialto Process*, *Minit* and *myInvenio* [5]. However, these tools could either not represent noise/outliers, could not compare *de jure* and *de facto* processes or showed limitations regarding the analysis of meta data, so we developed our own tool *SCCH Process AnT* (see Sect. 5). Nevertheless, a process mining tool is not the solution for everything; it supports process analysis but every analysis still requires various manual activities as described in the following section.

4   Business Scenarios

In this section, two business scenarios are presented taken from actual production processes of manufacturing companies. The first company already managed business processes, i.e. *de jure* process models were defined and considered in production. However, production also required decisions and allowed some degree of freedom, e.g., due to the quality of raw material. In sum, 21 different production processes with an overall amount of 1.5 million instances and 45.8 million process steps were considered. All process steps were logged by the production machines and stored in an Oracle database. The second company had two production processes (no *de jure* process model was defined) with 72 thousand instances of the first product and more than 1 million instances of the second product. The data was also stored in an Oracle database.

The data required for process mining may originate from different sources, e.g., from machine logs, files, custom databases or ERP systems. Since data is typically provided by different (heterogeneous) data sources, it must be extracted, transformed and loaded (ETL) in a data warehouse. The data must be cleaned (incorrect and incomplete data) and stored using consistent data formats. The mandatory attributes required for every log entry include the case ID, event (production step) and a time-stamp. In one of the business scenarios, time-stamps were not stored for several events, so it was first necessary to save this information to later perform a process analysis.

In order to analyze processes, we defined the following procedure:

1. Identification of different production processes
2. Identification of product instances and production steps (events)
3. Data Extraction: from machines or (heterogeneous) databases
4. Data Analysis: schema, views, tables, time-stamp columns
5. Data Cleaning: incorrect and incomplete data
6. Event Log Analysis: frequency of instances and events
7. Process Identification: visualization of actual process
8. Process Analysis: discussion of process with domain experts
9. Process Comparison: with *de jure* model (if existent)
10. Process Improvement: optimization potentials identified with domain experts

This procedure is not specific for production processes but can also be applied in other departments of a company (e.g., administration, logistics, goods receiving) and in further industrial sectors (e.g., banks, insurances, hospitals or public administration). The only requirement is that single items are considered like an insurance claim, a credit application or a produced item.

Considering the two business scenarios, we started the procedure by identifying production processes (step 1) and product instances/steps (step 2) based on a discussion with domain experts and on a visitation of the production facility. In both business scenarios, data was already transferred from production machines to Oracle databases (step 3). We then studied the data, searched for the main table of the process instance, considered relationships and identified time-stamp columns (step 4). Time-stamp columns are mandatory for every process step to provide a temporal ordering. Afterwards, we cleaned incorrect and incomplete data (e.g., null-values) (step 5) and defined corresponding views/tables with all production steps, the case ID, time values and (if existent) the product for each business scenario. We then analyzed the Event Logs with ProM (step 6) as shown in Fig. 2. However, due to confidentiality, data was anonymized, i.e. instead of product names and production steps a random abbreviation consisting of three letters was taken. We further used data extracts (e.g., for six months) to cope with data limitation in ProM. Figure 2 analysis 4502 instances and 89831 steps/events of one process. Figure 2(a) shows the dashboard with a visualization of steps per instance, e.g., minimum is 1 (probably process abortions), mean is 20, max is 49 (probably misbehavior with iterations), and Fig. 2(b) provides a summary with the absolute and relative occurrences of the 47 process steps and also their frequency as start- and end-events.

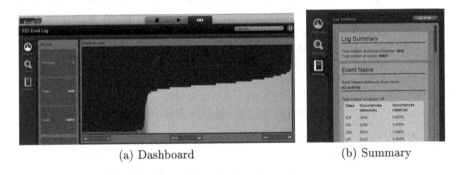

(a) Dashboard   (b) Summary

Fig. 2. Event log analysis

We further tried to identify the process (step 7) with ProM and used mining algorithms like *alpha-*, *heuristic-* and *fuzzy-miner*. However, the mining algorithms could not sufficiently fulfill the requirements. *Alpha miner* showed all process steps (graph nodes) and their ordering (graph edges) without any numbers or frequencies, so it was not possible to identify the main paths and distinguish them from outliers. *Heuristic-* and *fuzzy-miner*, on the other hand, filtered noise (outliers) and showed the frequency of the remaining paths. However, due to filtering, we could not study outliers, misbehavior and process abortions. Hence, we developed our own process analyzing tool and called it "SCCH Process AnT".

5   SCCH Process AnT

SCCH Process AnT supports three steps of the suggested procedure: Event Log Analysis, Process Identification and Process Comparison. The tool is implemented in Java and may process large data amounts (we encountered no limitations in the business cases). In addition, either the whole process may be displayed or thresholds can be set to filter noise. Further features of *SCCH Process AnT* are the possibility to display meta data (e.g., categorical (text) and numerical (decimal) classifications for attributes like costs, resources or status) as well as a comparison of *de jure* and *de facto* processes.

SCCH Process AnT provides a graphical user interface and may import data from csv-files or databases. The user then maps the columns to required analysis fields and configures the production process as well as a date/time range. Afterwards, the process is identified (possibly with a threshold) and shown in the graphical user interface (see Fig. 3(a)) as well as saved as graphml file. Next to every node, the mean execution time with standard deviation and meta data (in this case a categorical classification for resources and a numerical classification for costs) are displayed. Every edge is marked with the absolute and relative frequency and also comprises the mean waiting time with standard deviation. Figure 1(b) shows the *de facto* process model of the first business scenario for the product *GVU* with a threshold of 5% opened with the graph tool yEd (49 nodes/process steps and 76 edges). Figure 3(b) is much more complex (49 nodes and 995 edges), since it has no threshold set. This process analysis allows to study the outliers; it is possible to zoom into the process diagram and, e.g., to only display the neighbors of one node.

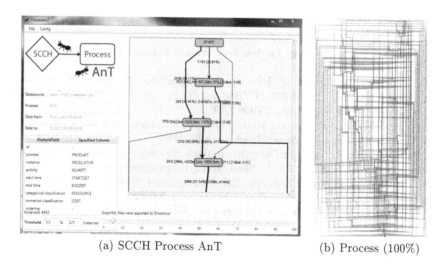

(a) SCCH Process AnT   (b) Process (100%)

Fig. 3. SCCH process AnT

So with *SCCH Process AnT* we mined all production processes (with and without thresholds) and, in case of the first scenario, we also showed meta data and automatically provided a comparison with the *de jure* process model. Optimization potentials are identified in the last step of the procedure and based on paths and time values. We considered infrequent paths, which may indicate outliers and misbehavior, as well as paths connecting a process step with the artificial end-event (may represent process abortions). Furthermore, considering time values, long waiting times are an evidence for bottlenecks and execution times with a high standard deviation indicate improvement potential. Finally, we optimized the processes together with domain experts of the companies.

6   Conclusion

Summing up, we suggested a procedure and a tool for process analysis and applied them in two actual projects of manufacturing companies. Although we focused on production processes, the suggested concepts are general enough to be also applied in other domains. Requirements of the process analysis were to also show less frequent process paths (outliers, abortions and misbehavior), to analyze large data amounts with possibly heterogeneous databases, and provide a detailed representation of time values and meta data. *SCCH Process AnT* can fulfill the requirements mentioned above, is developed with good performance, supports a comparison of *de jure* and *de facto* models and analyses meta data. The tool will be extended in future projects with further mining algorithms and representation forms (e.g., including statistics within a dashboard) as well as with additional functionality for process simulation and prediction.

References

1. Robertson, B.: Hype cycle for business process management. Technical report G00277213, Gartner (2015)
2. van der Aalst, W.M.P., et al.: Process mining manifesto. In: Daniel, F., Barkaoui, K., Dustdar, S. (eds.) BPM 2011. LNBIP, vol. 99, pp. 169–194. Springer, Heidelberg (2012). doi:10.1007/978-3-642-28108-2_19
3. van der Aalst, W.M.P.: Process Mining: Discovery, Conformance and Enhancement of Business Processes. Springer, Heidelberg (2011)
4. Wen, L., Wang, J., Sun, J.: Detecting implicit dependencies between tasks from event logs. In: Zhou, X., Li, J., Shen, H.T., Kitsuregawa, M., Zhang, Y. (eds.) APWeb 2006. LNCS, vol. 3841, pp. 591–603. Springer, Heidelberg (2006). doi:10.1007/11610113_52
5. van der Aalst, W.M.P.: Process Mining: Data Science in Action. Springer, Heidelberg (2016)
6. Natschläger, C.: Towards a BPMN 2.0 ontology. In: Dijkman, R., Hofstetter, J., Koehler, J. (eds.) BPMN 2011. LNBIP, vol. 95, pp. 1–15. Springer, Heidelberg (2011). doi:10.1007/978-3-642-25160-3_1
7. Kossak, F., Illibauer, C., Geist, V., Kubovy, J., Natschläger, C., Ziebermayr, T., Kopetzky, T., Freudenthaler, B., Schewe, K.D.: A Rigorous Semantics for BPMN 2.0 Process Diagrams. Springer, Cham (2015)

8. Kossak, F., Illibauer, C., Geist, V., Natschläger, C., Ziebermayr, T., Freudenthaler, B., Kopetzky, T., Schewe, K.D.: Hagenberg Business Process Modelling Method. Springer, Cham (2016)

9. Bögl, A., Natschläger, C., Karlinger, M., Schrefl, M.: Exploiting process patterns and process instances to support adaptability of dynamic business processes. In: 25th International Workshop on Database and Expert Systems Applications. CPS (2014)

10. Bögl, A., Natschläger, C., Geist, V.: Towards flexibility in business processes by mining process patterns and process instances. In: Modelsward. Scitepress (2016)

11. Castellanos, M., de Medeiros, A., Mendling, J., Weber, B., Weijters, A.: Business process intelligence. In: Information Science Reference, 456–480 (2009)

12. McCoy, D.W.: Business activity monitoring: calm before the storm. Technical report ID Number LE-15-9727, Gartner (2002)

13. Han, H., Kamber, M., Pei, J.: Data Mining - Concepts and Techniques. Morgan Kaufmann, San Francisco (2011)

14. Rozinat, A., van der Aalst, W.M.P.: Decision mining in ProM. In: Dustdar, S., Fiadeiro, J.L., Sheth, A.P. (eds.) BPM 2006. LNCS, vol. 4102, pp. 420–425. Springer, Heidelberg (2006). doi:10.1007/11841760_33

15. Darnton, G.: Business Process Analysis: Including Architecture, Engineering, Improvement, Management, and Maturity. Requirements Analytics, Bournmouth (2012)

IT-Trends

Master Data Quality in the Era of Digitization - Toward Inter-organizational Master Data Quality in Value Networks: A Problem Identification

Thomas Schäffer[1] and Christian Leyh[2(✉)]

[1] Faculty of Business Administration, University of Applied Sciences Heilbronn,
Max-Planck-Straße 39, 74081 Heilbronn, Germany
thomas.schaeffer@hs-heilbronn.de
[2] Chair of Information Systems, esp. IS in Manufacturing and Commerce,
Technische Universität Dresden, Helmholtzstr. 10, 01069 Dresden, Germany
christian.leyh@tu-dresden.de

Abstract. Increased digitalization in business and society has prompted drastic changes in companies, and at present, nearly all enterprises face enormous external and internal challenges to staying competitive. One such challenge concerns data quality in various enterprise systems, within both enterprises and entire value networks. Since data will continue to be the foundation of the digital economy, a certain level of data quality is necessary to ensure efficient business processes. Therefore, adequate master data quality management is essential at both the corporate and inter-organizational levels. In response, in light of a systematic literature review and interview study with several business experts experienced in and responsible for master data management in their companies, we not only underscore the need for research on inter-organizational master data quality, but also ultimately derive initial functional requirements for tools that can support inter-organizational information sharing in a value network.

Keywords: Data quality · Information sharing · Inter-Organizational business process · Master data · Value network · Supply chain

1 Motivation

"It is not too much of a stretch to think we have entered a golden age of digital innovation. Owing to the 50-year march of Moore's Law, we have witnessed the creation of a relatively cheap and increasingly easy-to-use world-wide digital infrastructure of computers, mobile devices, broadband network connections, and advanced application platforms" [1]. As the above quotation emphasizes, the advanced digitization of industry and commerce, as well as the further integration of smart objects toward merging the physical and digital worlds, seems to have resulted in new fundamental paradigm shifts.

Among the most important challenges that companies currently face is the digitization of business processes and of enterprises themselves. Companies have to engage global digital networking, improve the automation of individual and, at times, all

© Springer International Publishing AG 2017
F. Piazolo et al. (Eds.): ERP Future 2016, LNBIP 285, pp. 99–113, 2017.
DOI: 10.1007/978-3-319-58801-8_9

business processes, and re-engineer existing business models to generate momentum for digital innovation. Areas affected by such changes are diverse, including enterprise resource planning (ERP) systems or similar company-wide enterprise systems to achieve holistic support, and the planning of business activities throughout companies and across organizational borders, all amid the increasing interconnectedness of classical horizontal value chains to complex value networks. Another concern with continued digitization in enterprises is data quality in various enterprise systems within enterprises themselves and along their supply chains. More today than in the last decade, to become and stay competitive in the global business environment, companies have to exchange large amounts of data on an automated basis between internal departments and across organizational borders with business partners. Therefore, a certain level of data quality is necessary to ensure efficient company-wide and inter-organizational business processes [2–4].

Additionally, the rapidly increasing capacity of enterprise software and the associated decline in equipment costs per unit allow large, cross-linked networking both inside and outside companies. Therefore, companies have to ensure the quality of respective data within different digital programs. Innovative business models derived from the digitization effects require an active management of data quality in enterprises [5–7], which becomes even more important given that, despite numerous past efforts toward system consolidation, today's businesses struggle with quite heterogeneous, complex software landscapes consisting of different software system types and components (e.g., CRM, SRM, SCM, and function-oriented components) and challenging integration requirements. Thus, a trend toward more architectural flexibility regarding enterprise systems and a certain rejection of strongly integrated approaches is clear [8]. Amid the variety and interconnectedness of the software landscape of an enterprise itself and within the entire value network of companies, data quality becomes an essential and critical factor, especially since poor quality or errors within data can affect many different systems and companies [9]. For example, in a case study at a German consumer goods manufacturer Hüner et al. [10] found that data quality is a critical success factor for efficient inter-organizational collaboration. They identified and analyzed problems resulting from defects of product master data in inter-organizational business processes.

However, the lack of research dealing with the quality of data exchanged between organizations was already pointed out in 2009 by de Corbière [11]. Addressing this research gap, several authors [12–14] found that standards for product identification and classification and data pools have not gained wide acceptance in many industries because they do not meet key requirements of trading companies. Furthermore, Kauremaa et al. [15] showed that the RosettaNet standard alone was insufficient for creating system-to-system integrations. Even for the wide-spread data exchange standard EDI, Vermeer [16] pointed out that EDI requires a higher degree of context alignment between the sender and receiver of the EDI messages. If this higher degree of context data quality is not established, EDI will lead to a negative impact on process performance because the poor data quality in the context leads to more errors or more prevention in the ordering process. In addition, Dalmolen et al. [12] showed that data quality is crucial for collaboration success; however, there is much space for improvement. They stated that the use of a standard alone is insufficient. Success of product information sharing between suppliers and retailers largely depends on knowledge and skills of the people using the standard, and especially on the quality of product master data. This is also supported by Legner and Schemm [17] through examining product master data exchange in two retailer-manufacturer relationships. They conclude that industry standards do not fully cover inter-organizational coordination requirements.

Regarding these aspects, statements and findings, we set up a pre-study [18] focusing on master data quality and master data quality management in German enterprises. That study was conducted in the spring and early summer of 2015 with 254 companies and yielded two core findings:

First, regarding the **changed awareness of data quality**, 80% of companies assessed the impact of poor master data quality to be high or very high for their economic success. At the same time, 84% of companies rated the cost of ensuring master data quality as high or very high, and 71% of companies reported that the greatest challenge for data quality management was manual maintenance. Therefore, it is unsurprising that 82% of companies actively engage data quality initiatives. However, using appropriate methods eschews the systematic determination and improvement of master data quality. On that point, only 15% of companies knew those methods, mentioned for example by [19], and only 6% of companies, mostly large ones, used them. That phenomenon underscores the discrepancy between research and practice, which could be helped by reducing the complexity of the most scientific methods, including AIMQ [20], IQM or DQA, and providing appropriate best practices. Second, regarding the digitization of changed data quality management, digitization is based on a **profound linking of all business partners** in a supply chain and requires the actions of enterprise-wide and **inter-organizational master data quality**. Approximately 50% of companies studied expected to face the issue of digital business transformation in its different facets in the near future. In that sense, companies have indeed performed the first steps of internal master data management and intend to operationalize it later. However, 76% of companies believe that it is crucial that increasingly more data must be processed in less time and without error, even beyond company boundaries, since efficient and effective digitization of the entire value network relies on trust.

Summing up the statements from the several authors and the results of our pre-study, it can be stated that during the course of digitization, a company will hardly be able to escape the constantly increasing volume of data, in terms of both diversity and rate of change. Consequently, in the future, no company will be able to afford poor data quality in the course of the ongoing digitization. In that light, the correct assessment of existing data quality is a critical factor of successful business strategies. To counter the resulting complexity of data enlargement, companies' data processing tasks (e.g., creating, processing, and exchanging master data and measuring and managing data quality) need to be largely automated, and companies have to establish new approaches for inter-organizational information sharing [21]. In response, this paper presents first practical insights into the relevance of the issues addressed and initial proposals for solutions for inter-organizational information sharing. That discussion yields the primary research question of the paper: *How do the requirements of master data quality change in the context of digitization, especially in inter-organizational information sharing?*

We thus conducted a study to gain deeper insights into the issues and challenges of corporate-wide and inter-organizational master data quality. To that end, we performed 33 expert interviews to identify influential factors for ensuring high master data quality in information sharing between companies. In all, we follow a research approach similar to that of [22], who studied barriers to master data quality. We adapted their approach to include several steps, as shown in Fig. 1.

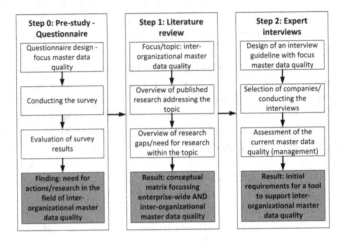

Fig. 1. Overview of the research process

To answer the research question, we present the results of the literature review (Step 1) and selected results of the study (Step 2). Likewise, the paper is structured as follows. After this section addressing our motivation for the research, we describe basic information about the key terms used. Next, in Sect. 3, we describe our literature review design and sum up the respective results found in the literature. Afterward, we present the interview study design and explain selected findings before discussing them in light of the research question. We end the paper with an outlook for future research in the field.

2   Conceptual Background

2.1   Master Data Quality

The concept of master data quality is not clearly defined in the literature, but derived from the combination of two concepts: master data and data quality. Master data consists of attributes that describe the core business objects of a company and form the basis for both the operational value-creation processes and analytical decision-making processes in the company. Master data refers to statistical data for goods, orders, products, employees, and similar objects that rarely undergo changes [22]. Typical master data classes are vendor master data, customer master data, and article or material master data [23]. Because they play an important role in the course of business process automation and data analysis, ensuring the high data quality of master data is especially important [24]. In that context, data quality is "a measure of the adequacy of the data for specific requirements in business processes, in which they are used. Data quality is a multidimensional, contextual concept, as it cannot be described with a single feature, but on the basis of different data quality dimensions and measures" [25]. In that respect, data quality is also often associated with the term "fitness for use" [26]. The most important dimensions for determining data quality are timeliness, consistency, accuracy, availability, and integrity [27].

2.2 Inter-organizational Business Processes

Inter-organizational business processes are sets of logically related tasks spanning more than a single organization [28] performed to achieve defined business outcomes [29]. The increasing importance of supply chains and value networks in combination with the consequent weakening of traditional corporate boundaries requires a comprehensive transformation of the coordination mechanisms used by business cooperation partners. Thus, inter-organizational business processes, in contrast to internal company processes, are defined by cut points resulting from companies' boundaries. Caused by these cut points, friction losses are fundamentally generated. To keep friction losses as low as possible and to ensure efficient process flows on an inter-organizational level, detailed coordination and communication between business partners becomes crucial. Inter-organizational cooperation processes need to ensure a correct bilateral flow of data along the supply chain and within the entire value network.

2.3 Value Networks

Christensen and Rosenbloom [30] coined the term value network, which they defined as a nested system consisting of a vertical and horizontal network structure. Peppard and Rylander [4] define a value network as a "value-creating system ... within which different economic actors – supplier, partners, allies, and customers – work together to co-produce value."

3 Literature Review

As part of our research approach (Fig. 1), we conducted a systematic literature review to determine the state of the art of research on master data quality at the inter-organizational level. For nearly all research approaches, a systematic literature review should be conducted to acknowledge current research activities and initiatives and to discern in what areas more results are needed or where research gaps exist [31]. To paint a holistic, complete picture on the object of study, a rigorous design is needed [32]. Therefore, for our literature review, we adopted the framework of [33], who have proposed five important phases for a rigorous literature review: (1) Definition of the object of investigation; (2) Conceptualization of the topic; (3) Literature search; (4) Literature analysis and synthesis; (5) Research agenda.

Into those phases, we integrated the suggestions of [32], who recommend for literature analysis the creation of a conceptual matrix to obtain an overall view on the topic. Our literature review was conducted as follows:

(1) Definition of the object of investigation:

An object of investigation should be identified, focused, on the one hand, on research results and, on the other, on other companies that might apply the results.

(2) Conceptualization of the topic:

The concepts of data quality management and coordination mechanism as described in Sect. 2 were used for conceptualization.

(3) Literature search:

The libraries were thought to cover mainstream information science sources and to reflect the information and data quality community. Therefore, four libraries were selected: Google Scholar (Google), IEEE Xplore Digital Library (IEEE), SpringerLink (SL) and AIS Electronic Library (AIS). Additionally, we performed a forward and backward search in relevant articles to identify further sources which could not be found by keyword search. During the search of literature within the four libraries, the terms were "master data quality" (MDQ), "master data management" (MDM) and "data quality management" (DQM). A similar approach was used by [34] in their analysis of information and data quality in business networking. The search yielded 155 papers, all of which were analyzed further. The selection of relevant articles was processed in two steps. At first, the abstract, introduction and conclusion of all papers

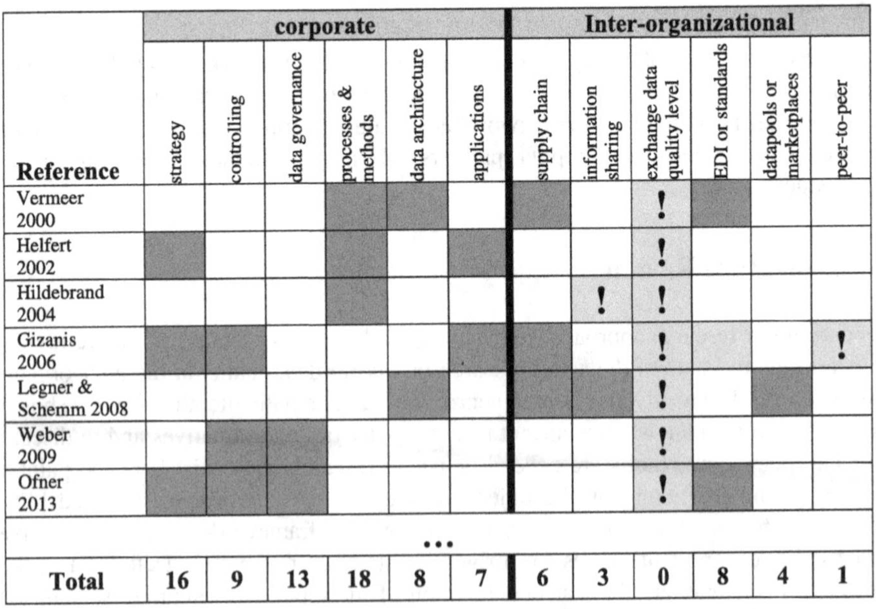

Reference	corporate						Inter-organizational					
	strategy	controlling	data governance	processes & methods	data architecture	applications	supply chain	information sharing	exchange data quality level	EDI or standards	datapools or marketplaces	peer-to-peer
Vermeer 2000									!			
Helfert 2002									!			
Hildebrand 2004								!	!			
Gizanis 2006									!			!
Legner & Schemm 2008									!			
Weber 2009									!			
Ofner 2013									!			
• • •												
Total	16	9	13	18	8	7	6	3	0	8	4	1

Fig. 2. Matrix corporate and inter-organizational MDQ

were reviewed. An article was accepted if it fulfilled the corporate and inter-organizational criteria. Forward and backward search brought 9 additional articles. The final set of 44 articles was then transformed into a concept-centric (Fig. 2) representation recommended by [32] and discussed in what follows.

(4) Literature analysis and synthesis:

Intra-organizational issues of ensuring and maintaining quality of master data have gained extensive attention in the literature [25, 26, 35]. However, achieving an adequate level of master data quality in inter-organizational business processes – particularly in product information sharing – has been given less attention as pointed out by [12, 13, 17, 36].

In most publications addressing the improvement of data quality in corporate contexts, a multidisciplinary approach is typically lacking [37]. No comprehensive methods are available to measure the quality of data and improve it, nor is any exact definition or metric that allows measuring enterprise-wide master data quality [20].

De Corbière [36] explored data quality dimensions that retailers and manufacturers consider to be relevant for the exchange of product information. He explains how adoption of inter-organizational information systems may contribute to product data quality improvement! However, the industry standard for exchanging information between enterprises furthermore lacks information about the data quality required [38]. An extension of the internal modeling method of business processes from the perspective of the data quality of current corporate contexts to an intercompany scenario is another important research topic [39]. The concept of measuring the quality of data in data warehouse systems in operational business processes and enterprise-wide information and logistics systems thus needs expansion [40]. Therefore, Otto et al. [41] address the challenge of managing the complexity of the data resource in the networked industry and encourage further research into more studies in the field.

Summing this up, despite the extensive attention towards data quality in the literature, research focusing inter-organizational aspects of master data quality has given only less attention as also stated in the motivation section.

(5) Research agenda:

Altogether, the results of our literature review show that research on master data quality adopts company-internal and cross-company perspectives. Heretofore, data quality research activities have focused predominantly on corporate (i.e., internal) master data quality. Nevertheless, a variety of methods, approaches, and solutions exist to evaluate and improve internal master data quality [19]. Those approaches are essential for enterprise-wide information management. The literature analysis also shows that the field of inter-organizational master data quality, despite its importance, is addressed by very few studies, which has resulted in a large gap in research on inter-organizational data quality management (see "!" in Fig. 2). From that, it can be stated in light of requirements for digitization, as stated in the motivation section and supported by our pre-study [18], that research on inter-organizational master data quality is needed. To gain a deep understanding of whether the concept is truly important for enterprises, we organized an interview study with business experts focusing on inter-organizational master data quality management. The approach and selected results from the study are shown in the next section.

4 Interview Study

The aim of the interview study was to provide insight into the relevance of inter-organizational master data quality from a practical business perspective. To that end, we first responded to indications provided in the pre-study [18] and the gap identified within our literature analysis and confronted business experts with those results and assumptions. The primary focus and questions of the interview study were: (1) "What problems and challenges of inter-organizational business processes exist regarding master data quality?" (2) "What requirements can be derived to determine and measure inter-organizational master data quality?"

4.1 Methodology

To gain insight into enterprise-wide, but especially inter-organizational master data quality, and their related challenges, we used a qualitative approach that involved organizing an exploratory study [42] consisting of 33 interviews with business experts experienced in and responsible for master data management in their companies. With this approach, we were able to delve deeper on the key findings in order to bring out more insights that can emerge from the interview data. The interview data should serve to inform what outcomes are being experienced from current practices. Therefore, this approach leads to a deeper understanding about the need for organizations for managing master data quality.

The selection of experts followed no formal rules and did not aim to fulfill the condition of representativeness. Instead, companies were selected from various sectors and of various sizes to gain broad insights into the topic. Expert interviews were conducted in the form of semi structured interviews. Interview guidelines were created based on the results of a pretest with several business experts. The guidelines consist of 18 questions in four primary parts: (1) General questions to ascertain experts' experience and their companies; (2) Questions about corporate master data quality; (3) Questions about inter-organizational master data quality; (4) Questions about future fields of action regarding master data quality. The guidelines were delivered to the interviewees one week prior to interviews, which occurred from August 2015 to February 2016. A total of 33 experts were interviewed. Interviews lasted from 42 to 125 min. Interviews were recorded electronically with the consent of the experts, and afterward, the content was analyzed according per the recommendations of [43]. A detailed list of the 33 expert interviews and the complete interview guidelines are available upon request.

4.2 Characterization of Participants

Table 1 provides an overview of experts interviewed and the industry affiliation of their companies. They take on the role of data user (dU) or data suppliers (dS). On the other hand, the data consultant group (dC) answered interview questions from the customer's perspective given their consulting experience in MDM and thus excellent insight into the companies' situations.

Table 1. Overview of interviewees by position

Position	dU/dS	dC
CIO/CTO	25% (8)	3% (1)
Head of Department (non IT)	12% (4)	–
Member of the MDM organization	12% (4)	–
Project manager MDM (business unit)	12% (4)	3% (1)
Project manager MDM (IT)	9% (3)	–
CEO	3% (1)	21% (7)

4.3   Corporate Master Data Quality

Answers to the question "How important is master data quality in your company?" show that each expert, whether a consultant or user, attests to the high or very high importance of high-quality master data (88%). Furthermore, most experts (82%) stated that master data have a high priority in the company and are regarded as an essential part of business processes. Furthermore, both groups generally reported that appropriate master data management prompts high master data quality, which in turn minimizes the risk of error and facilitates briefer, faster process cycles. Most experts (78%) also referred to master data as "company elixir," as one interviewee put it, that are essential for continuous, smooth processes within companies. According to the experts, in the course of digitization and increased networking among various business partners, the supply of high-quality master data along the value chain and in networks is crucial. One expert explained that a product exists only when it is electronically available with all of its features and when all corresponding data are correct.

In the Digital Age and amid the digital transformation involving the Internet of Things and Services and Industry 4.0, Big Data a high master data quality was reported to be essential. Supplying all points in the value network with valid and correct master data and in real time was argued to be an important challenge across

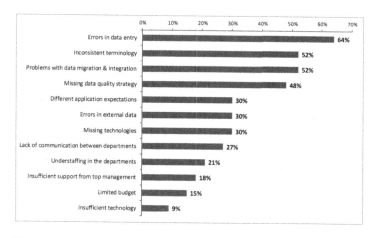

Fig. 3. Overview of master data problems in companies (multiple answer)

all industry sectors and companies regardless of size. Figure 3 illustrates the primary reasons for the companies' master data problems, which stem from strategic, operational, and technological areas. Strikingly, although 67% of companies represented in the interviews have already implemented measures to improve master data quality, the human factor (64.5%) was cited as the most common known reason for problems. According to the experts, there is a lack of automatic mechanisms for systematic error detection, of corporate data quality strategies and data governance, and of appropriate information sharing with business partners in value networks. In response, the goal of organizations should be fully automatic, corporate master data management that identifies master data problems as proactively as possible. Ideally, such master data management should also resolve problems or at least provide appropriate recommendations for necessary actions.

From those results, three core findings regarding corporate master data quality can be derived:

(1) As reported in all interviews, the assessment of MDQ is based mostly on summary assessment or gut feeling, not any systematic, method-supported quality determination that can be performed transparently and made available to all departments.

(2) Product and material master data are of especially high importance—as one interviewee put it, "Without electronic data, the product does not exist"—and subject to a continuous improvement pro. Therefore, the commerce sector has an even greater challenge given its wide range and number of products.

(3) Externally oriented core processes (e.g., procurement, purchasing, after-sales, and customer service) have a greater potential for improvement of master data quality than internally oriented ones. Overall, the companies represented lack a quality measurement for master data and do not engage departmental or enterprise-wide collaboration among semantic aspects (e.g., unified vocabulary).

4.4 Inter-organizational Master Data Quality

The overwhelming majority (87%) of experts expressed a view similar to that of study of [44], that a "shift of fixed value chains to dynamic value networks will evolve" (translated from [44]). Even more companies represented (94%) perform information sharing with business partners. In that context, master data usually mentioned are product and material master data (77%) and conditions or prices in sales (26%). According to the experts, information sharing is carried out at a volume of 80% on an electronic basis. Communication channels used differ and range from email (52%) to profound electronic data interchange (EDI) integrations (16%). Data content is structured in the form of Excel, CSV, or XML transfer (45%) or unstructured, as in PDF files (19%). Overall, the experts attested that quite a few standards for the exchange of master data, especially in the context of product information sharing, such as BMEcat, GS1, or ecl@ss, can be used.

According to most interviewees, the exchange, synchronization, and integration of master data with business partners are not smooth (55%). The reasons for that characterization are complex and diverse, yet can be classified in three primary categories: (1) lack of data management and organization; (2) lack of appropriate technologies and methods; (3) missing or unused standards. Among other important problems mentioned was the large volume of transferred data, whose quality cannot be ensured without sufficient methods and tools. Currently, in most companies represented, data quality is measured and determined manually and at random (81%), if at all. In general, a full analysis of incoming data sent from business partners is currently not performed. Errors due to incorrect master data are not initially detected, but only when the respective process displays an error, which has to be solved with an expensive reactive data correction.

Overall, the importance of master data quality is considered to be quite high throughout entire value networks. In contrast to that fact, the quality of master data received from both customers and suppliers, on average, was deemed of middling importance by interviewees; indeed, 42% of the experts assessed that quality as insufficient for accurate, automated process management in their companies. To improve that facet, the availability and use of tools with self-learning assessment rules and consistent standards and interfaces for system integration and information sharing are necessary, according to the experts. Interestingly, at that point, 58% of interviewed companies share with their business partners information about the extent, format, and quality of data for transmission. The ways in which such activity is performed differ greatly, starting with non-machine-readable communication by field service guidelines in the form of documents or Excel templates to given specific tools for information sharing. However, the subsequent examination of the master data supplied is not usually conducted. In that regard, 87% of the experts viewed the use of an auxiliary tool for inter-organizational master data quality management and measurement to be exceptionally useful.

4.5 Key Findings

Altogether, the following three key findings from the 33 expert interviews can be derived:

(1) The quality of internal master data bears great potential for improvement. One solution could be to establish corporate-wide data quality management.
(2) The quality of product information sharing among business partners remains insufficient and has great potential for improvement as well. One solution for this problem involves using basic technologies and standards such as BMEcat, EDI, SCOR, and data pools.
(3) Inter-organizational cooperation processes do not cover the specifics of respective companies and are not supported or conducted by all business partners in the same way. As a solution, bilateral consultations between companies are needed.

In light of the findings of the expert interviews, the following hypotheses can be derived:

Hypothesis 1: The higher the level of digitization, the greater the demand for high-quality master data and the greater the importance of implementing comprehensive master data quality management.

Hypothesis 2: The easier and more automated the use of a tool to determine inter-organizational master data quality, the greater the degree of its use and its results in the form of better quality master data.

5   Discussion and Future Aspects

As the previous sections have shown (i.e., the pre-study, literature review, and interview study), there is a reasonable need to address inter-organizational master data quality management. By conducting a systematic literature review, a research gap for this field could be identified. However, due to the ongoing, quickly evolving digitization of the global business environment, master data and their quality at internal and inter-organizational levels are crucial success factors for companies' success in cooperating in global value networks. Since data will continue to be the foundation of the digital economy, data need to be conceived as a strategic resource by companies that needs to be managed, especially in terms of time, costs and, above all, quality [25].

Digitization, (value) networking, and information supply have all prompted an ongoing, increasing volume of data in terms of range and rate of change. To respond to the resulting data complexity in an appropriate way, companies should provide automatic mechanisms for determining, assessing, and ensuring the quality of master data to the greatest extent possible. As such, specific software tools are mandatory, which can make a significant contribution, especially by enabling smaller companies to provide the necessary master data quality without investing millions and therefore help smaller companies to survive in the ongoing digital transformation of global business environments.

In sum, the analysis of the scientific literature and the results of the interview study reveal that although the research gap and great importance of inter-organizational master data quality and its management have been realized, no appropriate solutions have been presented, discussed, or even contemplated, which could nevertheless enable sufficient support for the problem. The very fact that experts were willing to participate in interviews that lasted 70 min on average shows that master data quality, especially in an inter-organizational context, is of incredible importance. Plus, nearly all experts signaled further interest and a willingness to probe more deeply into the field. Together with the experts, we derived some basic functional requirements for tools that can support inter-organizational master data quality and its management. Table 2 provides an overview of those requirements. However, no tool currently exists that covers the targeted requirements. A standard could be helpful, but do not represent company specifics or bilateral specifics of multiple companies in a dynamic value network [9, 11, 13, 15, 36]. In what follows, the usefulness and requirements of such a tool are discussed in light of statements made by interviewees. For one, the tool should be available and easy to handle for companies of all sizes, although especially smaller ones, which require many actions for master data management to be done manually without the support of tools. In that sense, the tool would be particularly interesting for medium-sized enterprises, given their lack of time, human resources, and expert knowledge. Activities of engineers employed could be replaced by automatic processes in reviewing master data quality or when troubleshooting. The tool would create transparency and trust as well as prompt process improvements, especially in terms of responsibility and liability. Today, a great deal of money and effort is spent because companies do not trust external master data from partners in the value network and therefore have to check those data manually. The tool could also ensure that ad hoc partners are involved in their own business partner network and across national borders, especially in the course of dynamic value networks. The tool could also be used in Industry 4.0/Industrial Internet contexts—for example, for automatic, smart communication between machines that negotiate which data will be exchanged, in what way, and of what quality.

Table 2. Overview of functional requirements for an inter-organizational MDQM tool

Module	Functionality
Analysis module	Construction of a comprehensive data warehouse
	Testing and simulation of data quality measurements and determinations
Cockpit	Visualization of master data quality against predefined indicators in the form of a cockpit for monitoring
Data model	Provision of specific vocabulary in a parent ontology manager
Rules engine	Automatic generation of business rules to validate, measure, and control master data quality
	Provision of data quality guidelines
	Provision of description languages for the rules
	Provision of best practice rules
Software architecture	Adherence to modular principle
	Adaptability
	Configurability
Software ergonomics	Ease of use in operations
	Understandability and comprehensiveness

The basic idea can be seen in the outsourcing of responsibilities to business partners to ensure that the data are approved and arrive with fewer or no errors due to being tested with appropriate (automatic) mechanisms. However, there is currently no tool available to fulfill those needs. It is also necessary for the tool to ensure inter-organizational master data quality and therefore for action and research, from both a scientific and practical perspective. At this point, the consequence is the continuation of our research activities. In concrete terms, that means: **(1)** Developing a conceptual framework for inter-organizational master data quality; and **(2)** Designing and conducting expert workshops to determine the functional requirements of such a tool for inter-organizational master data quality in greater detail and to a greater extent, in response to requirements encouraged by interviewees. Those workshops should be designed in light of specific, concrete cases and the processes of information sharing between real business partner companies.

References

1. Fichman, R.G., Dos Santos, B.L., Zheng, Z.: Digital innovation as a fundamental and powerful concept in the information systems curriculum. MIS Q. **38**, 329–343 (2014)
2. Pagani, M.: Digital business strategy and value creation: framing the dynamic cycle of control points. MIS Q. **37**, 617–632 (2013)
3. Sambamurthy, V., Bharadwaj, A., Grover, V.: Shaping agility through digital options: reconceptualizing the role of information technology in contemporary firms. MIS Q. **27**, 237–263 (2003)
4. Peppard, J., Rylander, A.: From value chain to value network: insights for mobile operators. European Manage. J. **24**, 128–141 (2006)
5. Otto, B., Weber, K.: Data governance. In: Hildebrand, K., Gebauer, M., Hinrichs, H., Mielke, M. (eds.) Daten- und Informationsqualität, pp. 277–295. Vieweg+Teubner, Wiesbaden (2011)
6. McKinsey Digital: Industry 4.0: How to navigate digitization of the manufacturing sector (2015)
7. Mathrani, S., Mathrani, A., Viehland, D.: Using enterprise systems to realize digital business strategies. J. Enterp. Inform. Manage. **26**, 363–386 (2013)
8. Bley, K., Leyh, C., Schäffer, T.: Digitization of German Enterprises in the Production Sector – Do they know how "digitized" they are? In: AMCIS 2016 Proceedings (2016)
9. Le Dû, A.-C., de Corbière, F.: IQ as an enabler of the green and collaborative supply chain. In: ICIQ 2011 Proceedings (2011)
10. Hüner, K.M., Schierning, A., Otto, B., Österle, H.: Product data quality in supply chains: the case of Beiersdorf. Electron Markets **21**, 141–154 (2011)
11. de Corbière, F.: Data quality and interorganizational information systems: the role of electronic catalogues. In: AMCIS 2009 Proceedings (2009)
12. Dalmolen, S., Moonen, H., van Hillegersberg, J.: Industry-wide inter-organizational systems and data quality. In: AMCIS 2015 Proceedings (2015)
13. Madlberger, M.: Can data quality help overcome the penguin effect? the case of item master data pools. In: ECIS 2011 Proceedings (2011)
14. de Corbière, F., Rowe, F.: Understanding the diversity of interconnections between IS: towards a new typology of IOS. In: ECIS 2010 Proceedings (2010)
15. Kauremaa, J., Nurmilaakso, J.-M., Tanskanen, K.: E-business enabled operational linkages. The role of RosettaNet in integrating the telecommunications supply chain. Int. J. Prod. Econ. **127**, 343–357 (2010)
16. Vermeer, B.H.: How important is data quality for evaluating the impact of EDI on global supply chains? In: HICSS 2000 Proceedings (2000)
17. Legner, C., Schemm, J.: Toward the inter-organizational product information supply chain. J. Assoc. Inf. Syst. **9**, 119–150 (2008)
18. Schäffer, T., Beckmann, H.: Trendstudie Stammdatenqualität 2016. Empirische Forschung zur aktuellen Situation der Stammdatenqualität in Unternehmen und daraus abgeleitete Trends zur digitalen Transformation. Steinbeis-Edition, Stuttgart (2016)
19. Batini, C., Cappiello, C., Francalanci, C., Maurino, A.: Methodologies for data quality assessment and improvement. ACM Comput. Surv. **41**, 1–52 (2009)
20. Lee, Y.W., Strong, D.M., Kahn, B.K., Wang, R.Y.: AIMQ. A methodology for information quality assessment. Inf. Manag. **40**, 133–146 (2002)
21. Otto, B., Ofner, M.H.: Strategic business requirements for master data management systems. In: AMCIS 2011 Proceedings (2011)
22. Haug, A., Stentoft Arlbjørn, J.: Barriers to master data quality. J. Enterp. Inf. Manage. **24**, 288–303 (2011)

23. Ofner, M., Straub, K., Otto, B., Oesterle, H.: Management of the master data lifecycle: a framework for analysis. J. Enterp. Inf. Manage. **26**, 472–491 (2013)
24. Wang, R.Y.: A product perspective on total tata quality management. Commun. ACM **41**, 58–65 (1998)
25. Otto, B., Österle, H.: Corporate Data Quality. Springer, Heidelberg (2016)
26. Wang, R.Y., Strong, D.M.: Beyond accuracy: what data quality means to data consumers. J. Manage. Inf. Syst. **12**, 5–33 (1996)
27. Morbey, G.: Data quality for desicion makers. A dialog between a board member and a DQ expert. Springer Gabler, Wiesbaden (2013)
28. Bakos, J.Y.: Information links and electronic marketplaces: the role of interorganizational information systems in vertical markets. J. Manage. Inf. Syst. **8**, 31–52 (1991)
29. Davenport, T.H., Short, J.E.: The new industrial engineering: information technology and business process redesign. Sloan Manage. Rev. **31**, 11–27 (1990)
30. Christensen, C.M., Rosenbloom, R.S.: Explaining the attacker's advantage. Res. Policy **24**, 233–257 (1995)
31. Cooper, H.M.: Organizing knowledge syntheses: a taxonomy of literature reviews. Knowl. Soc. **1**, 104–126 (1988)
32. Webster, J., Watson, R.T.: Analyzing the past to prepare for the future: writing a literature review. MIS Q. **26**, xiii–xxiii (2002)
33. vom Brocke, J., Simons, A., Niehaves, B., Riemer, K., Plattfaut, R., Cleven, A.: Reconstructing the giant. In: ECIS 2009 Proceedings (2009)
34. Otto, B., Lee, Y.W., Caballero, I.: Information and data quality in networked business. Electron. Markets **21**, 79–81 (2011)
35. Wand, Y., Wang, R.Y.: Anchoring data quality dimensions in ontological foundations. Commun. ACM **39**, 86–95 (1996)
36. de Corbière, F.: Interorganizational information systems and data quality improvement. In: ICIQ 2007 Proceedings (2007)
37. Hildebrand, K.: Datenqualität im supply chain management. In: Informatik 2004 Proceedings, pp. 239–243 (2004)
38. Schemm, J.W.: Zwischenbetriebliches Stammdatenmanagement. Lösungen für die Datensynchronisation zwischen Handel und Konsumgüterindustrie. Springer, Heidelberg (2009)
39. Ofner, M.H.: Datenqualitätsmanagement aus Prozessperspektive: Methoden und Modelle. St. Gallen (2013)
40. Helfert, M.: Planung und Messung der Datenqualität in Data-Warehouse-Systemen. St. Gallen (2002)
41. Otto, B., Abraham, R., Schlosser, S.: Toward a taxonomy of the data resource in the networked industry. In: 7th Intern. Scientific Symposium on Logistics, pp. 382–421 (2014)
42. Meuser, M., Nagel, U.: Das Experteninterview — konzeptionelle Grundlagen und methodische Anlage. In: Pickel, S., Jahn, D., Lauth, H.-J., Pickel, G. (eds.) Methoden der vergleichenden Politik- und Sozialwissenschaft. Neue Entwicklungen und Anwendungen, pp. 465–479. VS Verlag für Sozialwissenschaften, Wiesbaden (2009)
43. Mayring, P., Fenzl, T.: Qualitative Inhaltsanalyse. In: Baur, N., Blasius, J. (eds.) Handbuch Methoden der empirischen Sozialforschung, pp. 543–556. Springer VS, Wiesbaden (2014)
44. Bloching, B., Leutiger, P., Oltmanns, T., Rossbach, C., Schlick, T., Remane, G., Quick, P., Shafranyuk, O.: Die digitale Transformation der Industrie. Detailbetrachtungen von Roland Berger Strategy Consultants im Auftrag des Bundesverbands der Deutschen Industrie e.V. (BDI). München (2015)

Towards Differentiating Business Intelligence, Big Data, Data Analytics and Knowledge Discovery

Nedim Dedić[(✉)] and Clare Stanier

Faculty of Computing, Engineering and Sciences,
Staffordshire University, College Road, Stoke-on-Trent ST4 2DE, UK
nedim.dedic@research.staffs.ac.uk, c.stanier@staffs.ac.uk

Abstract. Confusion, ambiguity and misunderstanding of the concepts and terminology regarding different approaches concerned with analysing massive data sets (Business Intelligence, Big Data, Data Analytics and Knowledge Discovery) was identified as a significant issue faced by many academics, fellow researchers, industry professionals and domain experts. In that context, a need to critically evaluate these concept and approaches focusing on their similarities, differences and relationships was identified as useful for further research and industry professionals. In this position paper, we critically review these four approaches and produce a framework, which provides visual representation of the relationship between them to effectively support their identification and easier differentiation.

Keywords: Business Intelligence · Big Data · Data Analytics · Knowledge Discovery

1 Introduction

During our academic and industry based work, we identified an issue faced by many academics, fellow researchers and domain experts – namely confusion, ambiguity and misunderstanding of the concepts and terminology regarding the different approaches that are concerned with analysing massive data sets. For example, during the development and validation of a framework for Business Intelligence (BI), we were asked why we omitted concepts, such as Big Data (BD), Data Analytics (DA) and Knowledge Discovery (KD) from the proposed framework. Such questions are justified as there is no generally accepted unified standard or framework encompassing the fields of BI, BD, DA and KD, which we collectively define as a *cluster of concepts concerned with analysing massive data.* Although these and similar questions may be outside the scope of a particular research project, it can require additional time and effort to answer them, especially in a research context as discussion has to be based on analysis of the existing literature.

The literature evaluated in this paper, typically deals thoroughly with each of elements from the *cluster of concepts concerned with analysing massive data* but approaches the topic from specific perspectives. If treated at all in the literature, issues such as possible confusion, ambiguity and misunderstanding of concepts and the interrelations between

© Springer International Publishing AG 2017
F. Piazolo et al. (Eds.): ERP Future 2016, LNBIP 285, pp. 114–122, 2017.
DOI: 10.1007/978-3-319-58801-8_10

approaches, are treated only superficially, and are mostly focused on differentiation between BD and BI concepts from data structure perspective.

Thus, we identified a need to critically evaluate the *cluster of concepts concerned with analysing massive data.* The aims of this position paper are: (i) to critically examine and review BI, DA, BD and KD to identify disparities, similarities and relationships each to another, (ii) to provide "a tool" in the form of graphical representation to be used by other researchers to quickly respond to the issues, questions and problems based on misunderstanding of the concepts concerned in this paper, (iii) to create a base for, and to provoke further discussion, between researchers and scientists, and (iv) to propose an initial conceptual framework, which will support further research and enable easy identification and differentiation of the concepts and approaches discussed in this paper.

The rest of this paper is structured as follows: in Sect. 2, we review BI, in Sect. 3 we review DA and BD and Big Data Analytics (BDA) and in Sect. 4 we discuss KD. We identify the similarities, differences and relationships between concepts and approaches. In Sect. 5, we present the framework shown in Fig. 1 and discuss the validation approach.

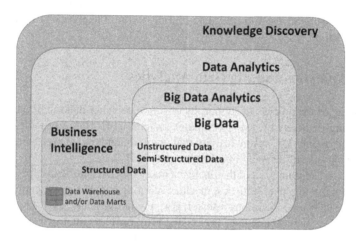

Fig. 1. Visual representation of the relationships between approaches

2   Business Intelligence

BI can be understood as a philosophy, which includes the strategies, processes, applications, data, products, technologies and technical architectures used to support the collection, analysis, presentation and dissemination of business information [1, 34]. It helps companies to out-think the competition through better understanding of the customer base [2], which could lead to creating a closer and stronger relationship with customers and enhanced revenue [3]. It plays a critical role for business in terms of organizational development by providing competitive advantage in the context of achieving positive information asymmetry [1, 4, 5], and contributes to optimising business processes and resources, maximizing profits and improving proactive [6], and strategic decision-making [7].

Besides its strategic and tactical advantages, Business Intelligence is also used at operational level.

BI could enable various types of users to spot emerging trends, make faster decisions, take actions and cope with the organizational problems as soon as they arise [8]. Its purpose is to help stakeholders to better understand their organization's operations, make wiser, more informed business decisions, and manage operational performance [9].

We can use BI to extract meaningful information and hidden knowledge from operational data produced on a daily basis, which would help business stakeholders in variety of predictions, calculations and analysis [10]. Conventional BI focused on activities such as ETL, data warehousing and reporting, thus covering research areas of data manipulation, propagation and visualisation [34]. However, the new generation of BI has an additional research focus on areas such as data exploration and visualisation [11, 12, 34]. There is also evidence of shifting from static reports to interactive visualisations, which extends research issues from metrics overview to discovering causes and effects of the phenomena the metrics express [12]. Additionally, the competition pressure of business causes new trends in BI and related research, such as near real-time BI, data mining and text analytics [13], self-service BI and BI in cloud [11].

3   Data Analytics and Big Data Analytics

Data Analytics is the process of supporting effective decision-making through analysis of the existing data sets by using computer systems [14]. Ridge provides a broader definition and defines DA as any activity that involves applying analytical processes to data for the purpose of deriving insight from data [15].

It is an interdisciplinary field that includes many other scientific disciplines, such as computational intelligence, statistics, machine learning, signal theory, pattern recognition, machine learning, operations research [14], predictive analytics, data mining, artificial intelligence, natural language processing [16], business intelligence, prescriptive analytics and descriptive analytics. As such, research areas and issues relevant for DA concepts include research areas and issues such as visualisation, cloud computing or data exploration, already identified as research areas in BI.

The mission of DA is to access and analyse data, and to gain insight into significant trends or patterns in organizations [17]. It provides managers with access to timely information and supports decision makers highlighting useful information [18]. As it supports advanced continuous monitoring and auditing [18], we can use it to examine various data sets to support operations in different industries [19]. It is also offers the opportunity, for example, to discover new customer segments, identify associated products, understand seasonal trends, or identify the quality of suppliers' [16].

DA is used by various industries, such as governmental organizations [18], healthcare, medicine [20], security [21], business, engineering, finance, operation management [22] and biomedical research [23].

3.1 Big Data

BD is concerned with large-volume, complex, ever growing data sets coming from various often autonomous sources [24], such as environmental and body sensors, mobile devices, administrative claims data, social media, emails, laboratory studies, electronic medical records, internet, business transactions, geospatial devices or sensors [22, 23, 25]. The rate of BD generation is extremely fast and BD may be generated by machines or humans [19]. Similar to Wu et al. [24] and Barton [23], many BD definitions and explanations are focused on the volume of data. However, BD is not only related to massive data [19], and there are other characteristics of BD, which are important and must be considered [16]. Traditional definitions of BD, include variety and velocity in addition to volume as basic constituent elements [16, 26]. Those three attributes are conventionally known as "three Vs".

Some definitions of BD go even further and include even more dimensions such as Veracity [25, 27, 28], Validity, Value, Variability, Venue, Vocabulary, and Vagueness [29] although the relevance of some of these elements is not clear. BD is everywhere around us [22]; in education [30], health care [23], engineering, operations managements, genomics [22], biomedical research [31] any many other fields.

However, massive and ever increasing data is useful only if it can be analysed [19]. Seen in the past as a technical problem, BD is today seen as a business opportunity [18], which can provide new opportunities based on the analysis of data [22]. The basic challenge of BD is to explore large data for the purpose of extracting useful information and competitive knowledge [32]. Unlocking the value of BD in complex and rapidly changing markets can bring competitive advantage and enable better response by businesses [25].

The definition of BD encompasses variety of data, which can be unstructured, semi-structured, and even structured. However, BD is most often concerned with unstructured and unorganized data [19, 23, 25, 27, 31].

On the other side, BI is mostly related to structured data, thus, we consider BD as a parallel philosophy to BI. However, this does not mean that they or their components are mutually exclusive. For example, DW as a core component of BI that works with structured data, can be used as additional part of the BDA process [25]. Notably, Chan [25] identified synergy between DW and Hadoop type BD architecture.

We identified quality and data exploration as the main research areas of BD and visualization as an important research area. Because of the size of the data considered, we see great potential in the research area of BD in the cloud.

3.2 Big Data Analytics

As traditional DA is not able to handle very large quantities of data [29], and because Big Data is too large and complex to be manipulated or managed by using standard tools and methods [26], we are witnessing a new trend - namely Big Data Analytics (BDA). BDA is defined as large-scale analysis and processing of information [22], encompassing data sets that go beyond the capacity of conventional databases [33]. It is advanced analytics operating with big data sets [16]. BDA is a rapidly expanding field [20]. We see BDA as similar to DA since BDA includes inspecting, cleaning, transforming, and modelling data to discover and communicate useful information and patterns, suggest conclusions, and support decision making, however, by using BD data sets [26].

BDA provides tools and methods to accumulate, manage, analyse, combine and assimilate large volumes of disparate, structured, and unstructured data [20, 25, 26]. Besides combining data, BDA sometimes requires combinations of various methods from different disciplines [26]. As its name suggests, BDA is concerned with Big Data and Analytics [16], and is a current research and application area [24]. As a concept related to BD, BDA is concerned with the same research areas as BD.

4   Knowledge Discovery and Data Mining

While applying appropriate tools and software [18], BDA uses various DA methods, such as clustering, classification, association rule or sequential patterns to discover new knowledge [29]. Methods and algorithms for analysing data and identifying patterns are collectively known as Data Mining (DM) [18, 22].

DM is considered a powerful approach for developing knowledge from data [35]. DM is understood as applying data analysis and discovery algorithms to produce a particular enumeration of models over existing data [36]. In this context, data exploration is the most relevant research area for DM.

Esfandiari et al. [35] state, in their reference to Fayyad et al. [36], that DM was originally considered as synonym for Knowledge Discovery in Databases (KDD). However, in the original text, Fayyad et al. [36] regard DM as a step in the KDD process, which includes application of specific algorithms for extracting patterns from data. Chen et al. [37] regarded DM and KD in databases as synonyms.

According to Fayyad et al. [36], KDD includes additional steps, which include data preparation, data selection, data cleaning, incorporation of appropriate prior knowledge, and proper result interpretation. We consider next what is understood under the heading of Knowledge Discovery (KD).

According Cortez & Santos [38], based on the 1996 definition by Fayyad et al. [36], KD is a branch of the artificial intelligence field that aims to extract high-level knowledge from complex and voluminous data, which would be useful and understandable. However, care is needed when using definitions from the period, which preceded BD. A 2004 definition by Koua & Kraak [39] defined KD as a higher-level process, which uses DM process to turn data into knowledge. More recently, 2009 [40] and 2011 [41], KD was defined not only as a branch of Artificial Intelligence, but as an interdisciplinary field with the focus on methodologies to identify valid, novel, meaningful and potentially useful patterns often from large data sets. We regard KD as a higher entity encompassing DA, which is not exclusively related only to computer-based concepts.

5 A Framework to Differentiate Business Intelligence, Big Data, Data Analytics and Knowledge Discovery

There are many similarities between BI, DA, BD and KD, which explains the confusion concerning these concepts. However, based on our literature review and preliminary discussions with seven domain experts, we identify significant differences and argue that these concepts should be regarded as distinct approaches.

As presented in Fig. 1, we see Knowledge Discovery as the highest-level concept, which in addition to other methods includes Data Analytics to discover or produce new knowledge. Within KD, we see Data Analytics as an entity, which includes various disciplines, including Big Data Analytics and Business Intelligence.

For the purposes of our discussion, which is focused on the analysis and use of data, we regard Big Data as part of Big Data Analytics. Taking into account intention, purpose and underlying business philosophies, we see Big Data Analytics and Business Intelligence at the same level. However, taking into account technical structure, relevant software applications and data, we also see Big Data and Business Intelligence as concepts at the same level.

We see data focus as the major difference between BI and Big Data. Big Data encompasses unstructured, semi-structured and structured data, however the main focus is on unstructured data [19, 23, 25, 27, 31], while the focus of BI is on structured data. While BI requires DW and/or data marts to support reporting [42, 43], Big Data can work with DW but DW are not required [25] and there are many alternative supporting technologies such as the Hadoop platform. In reports based on traditional BI systems, there is a requirement to have structured master and transactional data. For example, to use or analyse sales transactional data we must have master data describing the properties of sales (such as store, location or product descriptions). Big Data is not subject to those requirements. For example, the analysis of the content of emails or appeals submitted to public administration institutions does not require structured data.

5.1 Validation of the Framework Proposed

In the academic community, validation is usually based on approaches such as formal interviews or surveys. These approaches are time consuming for participants and we were interested to see whether professional networks could be used to gather responses. The concepts proposed in this paper are intended as discussion points and for this reason we wanted to reach out to the professional practitioner community, to evaluate whether the distinctions we propose match the real world experience of those working in the field. Thus in addition to online survey and direct discussion with domain experts, we used an additional method of communication, namely special interest groups on internet-based business social networks to discuss and validate the proposed framework. We exposed the framework from Fig. 1 to relevant domain experts for discussion as a post using appropriate LinkedIn groups.

To better understand the validation process, we explain which kinds of feedback are available in these forums. *Like* is the lowest level category feedback on content that a user can provide in internet-based business social networks. However, it has positive impact as it indicates that the user found the content interesting, useful or worth considering. *Comment* can be considered as a stronger category of feedback in regard to *like*. It is direct discussion about content, which can have positive or negative impact. It is also an appropriate mechanism for critically evaluating content and providing additional suggestions. *Share* can be considered as the strongest type of feedback in internet-based business social networks. It allows sharing of content on personal profiles of users called to provide feedback, in other groups, and in news feeds. By sharing respective content via internet-based business social networks, user suggests not only that respective content, concept or idea is interesting, useful or worth considering, but also worth promoting further within the community. *Share* may also have negative connotations but this was not the case in this work.

Over a period of three weeks, we received 560 feedbacks in three different forms. It was very encouraging that 384 users from business social networks found the framework good enough to be liked, while 134 decided to share the proposed framework with their professional networks as a good example explaining differences between BI, BD, DA and KD. Written comments were received from 42 users via preliminary survey and via business social networks; these comments were very positive and no negative comments were received. Suggestions for extending the framework included adding additional dimensions to the framework to categorize the type of analytics for each specific concept, such as descriptive, predictive, or prescriptive, and including concepts such as Machine Learning, Business Analytics, or Data Science. In our further work, we will review the framework and consider extending it to include additional elements.

References

1. Dedić, N., Stanier, C.: Measuring the success of changes to existing business intelligence solutions to improve business intelligence reporting. In: Tjoa, A.M., Xu, L.D., Raffai, M., Novak, N.M. (eds.) CONFENIS 2016. LNBIP, vol. 268, pp. 225–236. Springer, Cham (2016). doi:10.1007/978-3-319-49944-4_17
2. Brannon, N.: Business Intelligence and E-Discovery. Intellect. Property Technol. Law J. **22**(7), 1–5 (2010)
3. Alexander, A.: Case Studies: Business intelligence. Accounting Today, p. 32, June 2014
4. Marchand, M., Raymond, L.: Researching performance measurement systems: An information systems perspective. Int. J. Oper. Prod. Manage. **28**(7), 663–686 (2008)
5. Thamir, A., Poulis, E.: Business intelligence capabilities and implementation strategies. Int. J. Global Bus. **8**(1), 34–45 (2015)
6. Olszak, C.M., Ziemba, E.: Business Intelligence Systems in the holistic infrastructure development supporting decision-making in organisations. Interdisc. J. Inf. Knowl. Manage. **1**, 47–58 (2006)
7. Popovič, A., Turk, T., Jaklič, J.: Conceptual model of business value of business intelligence systems. Manage. J. Contemp. Manage. **15**(1), 5–29 (2010)
8. Sandu, D.I.: Operational and real-time Business Intelligence. Informatica Economic **XII**(4), 33–36 (2008)
9. American Institute of CPAs. (2015). Business Intelligence. http://www.aicpa.org/INTERESTAREAS/INFORMATIONTECHNOLOGY/RESOURCES/BUSINESSINTELLIGENCE/Pages/default.aspx. Accessed 27 Mar 2015

10. Kurniawan, Y., Gunawan, A., Kurnia, S.G.: Application of business intelligence to support marketing strategies: a case study approach. J. Theor. Appl. Inf. Technol. **64**(1), 214 (2014)
11. Obeidat, M., et al.: Business intelligence technology, applications, and trends. Int. Manage. Rev. **11**(2), 47–56 (2015)
12. Anadiotis, G.: Agile business intelligence: reshaping the landscape, p. 3 (2013)
13. Chaudhuri, S., Dayal, U., Narasayya, V.: An overview of business intelligence technology. Commun. ACM **55**(8), 88–98 (2011)
14. Runkler, T.A.: Data Analytics: Models and Algorithms for Intelligent Data Analysis, 1st edn. Springer Science & Business Media, Wiesbaden, Germany (2012)
15. Ridge, E.: Guerrilla Analytics: A Practical Approach to Working with Data. Morgan Kaufmann, Waltham (2014)
16. Russom, P.: TDWI Best Practices Report: Big Data Analytics (2011)
17. Lussier, R.N., Hendon, J.R.: Fundamentals of Human Resource Management: Functions, Applications, Skill Development, 1st edn. SAGE Publications, Los Angeles (2016)
18. Fadairo, S.A., Williams, R., Maggio, E.: Using data analytics for oversight and efficiency. J. Gov. Financ. Manage. **64**(2), 18 (2015)
19. Henry, R., Venkatraman, S.: Big Data analytics: the next big learning opportunity. Acad. Inf. Manage. Sci. J. **18**(2), 17–29 (2015)
20. Belle, A., Thiagarajan, R., Soroushmehr, S.M.R., Navidi, F., Beard, D.A., Najarian, K.: Big Data analytics in healthcare. BioMed Res. Int., 1–16 (2015). http://doi.org/10.1155/2015/370194
21. Cárdenas, A.A., Manadhata, P.K., Rajan, S.P.: Big Data analytics for security. IEEE Secur. Priv. **11**(6), 74–76 (2013)
22. Gerard, G., Haas, M., Pentland, A.: Big Data and management. Acad. Manag. J. **57**(2), 321–326 (2014)
23. Barton, A.: Big Data. J. Nursing Educ. **55**(3), 123–124 (2016). http://doi.org/10.3928/01484834-20160216-01
24. Wu, X., Zhu, X., Wu, G.-Q., Ding, W.: Data mining with Big Data. IEEE Trans. Knowl. Data Eng. **26**(1), 97–107 (2014)
25. Chan, J.O.: An architecture for Big Data analytics. Commun. IIMA **13**(2), 1 (2013)
26. Cao, M., Chychyla, R., Stewart, T.: Big Data analytics in financial statement audits. Account. Horiz. **29**(2), 423 (2015). http://doi.org/10.2308/acch-51068
27. Lokhande, S., Khare, N.: An outlook on Big Data and Big Data analytics. Int. J. Comput. Appl. **124**(11), 37–41 (2015). http://doi.org/10.5120/ijca2015905658
28. IBM. The Four V's of Big Data (2016). http://www.ibmbigdatahub.com/infographic/four-vs-big-data. Accessed 13 Apr 2016
29. Tsai, C.-W., Lai, C.-F., Chao, H., Vasilakos, A.: Big Data analytics: a survey. J. Big Data **2**(1), 1–32 (2015). http://doi.org/10.1186/s40537-015-0030-3
30. Metz, S.: Big Data. Sci. Teach. **82**(5), 6 (2015)
31. National Institutes of Health. What is Big Data? (2016). https://datascience.nih.gov/bd2k/about/what. Accessed 13 Apr 2016
32. Rajaraman, A., Ullman, J.D.: Mining of Massive Datasets, 1st edn. Cambrige University Press, Cambrige (2011)
33. Nicol, D.: Mobile Strategy: How Your Company Can Win by Embracing Mobile Technologies, 1st edn. IBM Press, Boston (2013)
34. Dedić, N., Stanier, C.: An Evaluation of the challenges of multilingualism in data warehouse development. In: Proceedings of the 18th International Conference on Enterprise Information Systems, vol. 1, pp. 196–206 (2016)

35. Esfandiari, N., Babavaliana, M.R., Amir-Masoud, E.M., Tabarb, V.K.: Knowledge discovery in medicine: current issue and future trend. Expert Syst. Appl. **41**(9), 4434–4463 (2014). http://doi.org/10.1016/j.eswa.2014.01.011
36. Fayyad, U., Piatetsky-Shapiro, G., Smyth, P.: Knowledge discovery and data mining: towards a unifying framework. In: Proceedings of the 2nd International Conference on Knowledge Discovery and Data Mining, pp. 82–88. AAAI Press (1996)
37. Chen, M.-S., Han, J., Yu, P.: Data mining: an overview from a database perspective. IEEE Trans. Knowl. Data Eng. **8**(6), 866–883 (1996). http://doi.org/10.1109/69.553155
38. Cortez, P., Santos, M.F.: Knowledge discovery and business intelligence. Expert Syst. **30**(4), 283–284 (2013)
39. Koua, E.L., Kraak, M.-J.: Geovisualization to support the exploration of large health and demographic survey data. Int. J. Health Geographics **3**(12), 13 (2004). http://doi.org/10.1186/1476-072X-3-12
40. Fred, A.: "Preface." Preface. In: International Conference on Knowledge Discovery and Information Retrieval. Madeira, Portugal (2009)
41. Aradau, C., Van Munster, R.: Politics of Catastrophe: Genealogies of the Unknown. Routledge, Chippenham (2011). http://www.kdir.ic3k.org/
42. Kimball, R., Margy, R., Thornthwaite, W., Mundy, J., Becker, B.: The Data Warehouse Lifecycle Toolkit, 2nd edn. Wiley, Indianapolis (2008)
43. Inmon, B.W.: Building the Data Warehouse, 4th edn. Wiley, Indianapolis (2005)

Significance of Quality 4.0 in Post Merger Process Harmonization

Irene Schönreiter[✉]

Technical University Dresden, Dresden, Germany
Irene@schoenreiter.de

Abstract. Industry 4.0 has received much attention in recent years, in parallel due to an increasing number of mergers and acquisitions (M&As), post merger integrations (PMI) is of continuous interest. Depending on the integration approach, process harmonization is vital during the PMI. The objective of this article is to observe the significance of Quality 4.0 during process harmonization and detect the extent of realization of this vision in service companies. A systematic literature review and empirical research with expert interviews have been executed. The research showed that Industry 4.0 is still a topic of enormous interest although there seems to be a gap between scientific publications and knowledge in practice. Especially towards Quality 4.0 and service companies future research is needed. In none of the service organizations are any intrinsic endeavors for implementing Industry 4.0 elements (e.g. ERP systems). A massive elucidation and information about Industry 4.0 in practice is demanded. Downstream markets could profit immense from the accompanied potential.

Keywords: Quality 4.0 · Industry 4.0 · Process harmonization · Post merger integration

1 Introduction

After mergers and acquisitions (M&A) companies are faced with the challenge to harmonize their processes and management systems. Process harmonization has to deal with two process variants that exist in parallel in the merged company parts. Depending on the integration approach the harmonization and standardization of processes can take extensive endeavors up to a completely new designed management system, whereas the single process itself should remain as simple as possible. Business processes can be simplified by the use of standardized supporting IS-Tools after an M&A [1]. A study of Mendling et al. (2016) demonstrates a high importance of digitalization in Business Process Management [2]. It is hypothetically assumed that process harmonization in post merger integration provides a worthy opportunity for a modernization with supportive IT systems and take strategically steps for the future. Binner (2014) emphasizes the importance of "information" as a new production factor in a process oriented organizational development. Information influences all technical aspects of a process [3].

The article at hand surveys the significance of Industry 4.0 for practioners, who are already challenged with the redesign of processes and management systems. It might be

© Springer International Publishing AG 2017
F. Piazolo et al. (Eds.): ERP Future 2016, LNBIP 285, pp. 123–134, 2017.
DOI: 10.1007/978-3-319-58801-8_11

obvious that the change situation in post merger integration motivates companies to redesign with Industry 4.0 elements and ensure processual success for the future – that means process harmonization with Quality 4.0 and corresponding IT systems. A separated consideration of organizational and technical solutions cannot be realized in process design [4]. Supportive IT solutions reach more process standardization and hence are more robust, effective and less prone to errors. Up to now experience with the execution of Big Data in service companies is still missing. Quality methods have to be checked on their readiness for Quality 4.0 and future consolidations and how the application can profit from the experiences in production industry [5]. To discover the strategy and motivation of practioners, in-depth-interviews with experts have been accomplished. All experts are/were personally involved in the process harmonization after an M&A.

First of all there are two research questions (RQ) in this paper:

- RQ1. Has Industry 4.0 still the importance to be regarded as a relevant topic for companies?
- RQ2. Which significance has Industry 4.0 in process harmonization in the post merger integration phase?

This paper is structured into six sections. Next section discusses the theoretical background and related work. Afterwards there is a detailed description of the applied research method, which is based on a literature review according to vom Brocke et al. (2009) and Webster & Watson (2002) and empirical research with quantitative content analysis according to Mayring (2014, 2015). The results of both are presented and discussed in Sect. 5. This article finishes with concluding thoughts and suggestions for future research.

2   Related Work

"Industry 4.0" is the fourth industrial revolution. Mid of the 18th century began the industrial production by means of water and steam - the first industrial revolution. With the introduction of the assembly line by means of electrical energy, and thus the mass production in 1880 started - the second industrial revolution was activated [6]. The third industrial revolution started in the 1970s with the use of electronics and computers to automate and aimed at unmanned factory. Many of these goals were not fulfilled, so in 1990 this approach has been declared as failed. Currently we are at the beginning of the fourth industrial revolution (Industry 4.0) that aims to equip the German industry for the future of production and an advance on the way to the lead market of Cyber-physical systems [7]. The term "Industry 4.0" has first been formed in the Hanover fair 2011 [8]. *"Industry 4.0 is best understood as a new level of organizational control over the entire value chain of the life cycle of products, it is geared towards increasingly individualized customer requirements. The basis of the fourth industrial revolution is the availability of all relevant information in real time by connecting all instances involved in the value chain"* (translated from German) [9, 10].

The development in Germany is strongly supported by the Government that supports the project with up to € 200 million [11]. The focus is the compound of the virtualization of physical production and logistics processes, which mean the extensive connection of production techniques and automation islands that are communicated and optimized over the internet in real time. This change impacts the process maps of companies significantly and holds a number of possible errors [3]. At the same time, the importance of service quality remains high. In the growing homogenization of the service sector, a consistent customer orientation and assurance of a superior quality of service becomes even more essential, the spiral of expectations screws itself [12].

In the vision of Industry 4.0 each customer order or each component will control itself independently through the entire production process thanks to the extensive information in the ERP systems [13]. The close interaction between human and robot causes a process acceleration due to the versatility of a high flexibility, a significant reduction of complexity in planning and control as well as savings of approximately 20 per cent due to a significantly higher productivity [14]. Further according to a survey of VDE companies expect a greater flexibility, optimized processes, individualized products, fast realization of new products, cost savings and resource efficiency [15].

Quality 4.0 means the integration and synchronization of procedures in production and process assurance with connected actions to quality assurance [16]. Industry 4.0 requires from Quality 4.0 a strong focus on quality planning and control, quality assurance in the manufacturing 4.0 and quality gain through data recycling [17].

In general, the connection of operational data and quality management systems is too little linked. Via existing Enterprise Resource Planning systems (ERP) tons of data could be detected. In the best case the quality management systems manages this data diversity with the use CAQ (Computer Aided Quality) systems today [18]. To get CAQ-Systems ready for Quality 4.0 they have to be developed to a network of real-time analysis systems with data out of event-driven testing-schedules, ongoing process stability assessment of the complete production chain, with the aim to introduce countermeasures before any production stops or rejects are produced [16]. With these analysis out of automated operating figures and available information, engineering and product design are highly influenced and can be optimized, the involvement of suppliers and customers is needed [16].

In conclusion there is a high potential for business process improvements and management systems to use. Process harmonization in the post-merger integration might be a good start to give birth to the future management system. Process harmonization means the standardization of business processes and the process control via different organizational units and locations [19]. The process-oriented quality management system associates, manages and directs all activities in an organization, covering the requirements of the target groups by authoritative specifications for the company-specific processes [20].

Of course the degree of integration depends of the integration approach. Aside from post merger IT integration there is no identified methodology to harmonize processes in the post merger situation [5]. Post-merger integration refers to the integration of a company after the signing of a M&A in which the integration planning and implementation takes place in order to realize the desired appreciation successful [21]. According to the need for organizational autonomy and need for strategic interdependence, different types of integration approaches exist: absorption, symbiosis, preservation and holding [22–24].

- Absorption: the acquired company is absorbed by acquirer and assimilated into its culture, the management usually comes from the acquirer [25], completely new for the absorbed party [26],
- Symbiosis: evolution from existing [26], learn from each other and share qualities
- Preservation: acquired company retains independence, modest degree of integration by acquired company [25]
- Holding: integration is not intended, no risk-sharing, no general management capability [22]

For process harmonization are especially absorption and symbiosis of relevance.

3 Methodology

3.1 Scope and Search Process of Literature Review

A systematic literature review is used to identify the status quo of research results of Industry 4.0. This literature review follows the approach of a systematic concept-centric literature review of Webster and Watson´s and synthesizes and extends existing research. It intends to develop a conceptual model with supporting propositions [28]. The current development of Industry 4.0 is presented.

The scope is defined by the methodology of Coopers taxonomy [29]. The focus of the review concentrates on research outcomes and the goal remains on the identification of central issues in the interface of Industry 4.0 to process harmonization. The author takes up a neutral position and representation and intends to inform the reader about the results in a constructive manner [28]. The extent of this review is representative due to the intended presentation of a status quo of the temporary research development. The literature search process is executed in six databases and organized historically. This review is intended to give general perception of existing literature in the interface of Industry 4.0 and process harmonization, so the main audiences are general scholars.

The literature search process has been executed in the "OPACplus" database, "EconBIZ", "WISO", "Emerald" (search executed July 2016) as well as in "Scopus" and "Mendeley" (search executed November 2016) and has been documented according to vom Brocke et al. [30]. The search terms are "Industry 4.0/Industrie 4.0" and "Quality 4.0/Qualität 4.0", both terms have been searched in English and German language. The results have been narrowed down with keyword search only.

3.2 Qualitative Analysis

A qualitative analysis was used to identify the significance of Quality 4.0 and its expenditure in practice. A qualitative semi-structured interview has been conducted with experienced experts in process harmonization after M&A. The evaluation was performed by qualitative content analysis according to Mayring (2014, 2015) [31, 32]. Interviewing experts is aligned by specific problems and demand of a questionnaire and offers the interviewee an extended space for the answer [33], so the orientation is more subjective and interpretative [34].

Therefore eleven experts composed of CEOs/COOs (36%) and quality managers (64%) of different service sector companies of the branches software engineering, supplies & services, health, consulting, plant engineering and miscellaneous services have been interviewed. All of them have already controlled a PMI or were actively involved. They have been requested to give estimation for the importance of Industry 4.0 and Quality 4.0 in the course of process harmonization during the post-merger integration phase.

The interviews were conducted under neutral conditions and evaluated anonymously. However, reference should be made to possible distortions which can usually arise through the interviews. The interviews are liable to "artificial", so that the statements can differ from a "natural" situation outside the interview [35].

The reactivity results from a reactive interaction between the person of the interviewee and the interviewer and the resulting response distortions [36] (and can be expressed as follows:

- Consent-mindedness ("akquieszens"): the respondents tend to be unconcerned when cognitively over consuming the question, or react with meaninglessness [36, 37]
- social desirability response set: the respondent answers the question of social standards and his assessment of the interviewer´s expectation [35, 37].

Furthermore, the "selective failure" can lead to a falsification of the results [36]. Individuals with an explicit interest in the survey methodology tend to participate, contributing significantly to the return rate of a survey, while persons with less interest in the topic do not participate in the survey [35].

4   Results

4.1   Results of Literature Review

The literature search process resulted in 1.215 hits. After an analysis for general relevance the number could be reduced to 833 articles. In respect to a partly consideration of 2016, the following evaluation presents the average number of published articles per month. The absolute appearance of articles is following: 2012: 13 articles, 2013: 72 articles, 2014: 178 articles, 2015: 517 articles, 2016: 299 articles.

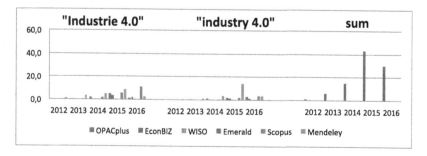

Fig. 1. Results literature review

The results show an impressing result of German articles (search term "Industrie 4.0) compared with English appearance (search term "Industry 4.0). This may be caused by the fact that the term's origin "Industry 4.0" is of German nature and outside Germany hardly known - although in content there are Industry 4.0 endeavors all over the world [38]. "Quality 4.0" is scarcely discussed in literature, the search result has shown only 30 relevant hits, so in the literature synthesis this part was no longer regarded.

Figure 1 shows he average number of publications per month from 2012 to 2016. The first publications appeared in 2012. There has been a sharp rise from 2013 to 2015.

4.2 Results of Qualitative Analysis

The result of the expert interviews is clear: for 91% of the interviewees Industry 4.0 has no significance during process harmonization (see Fig. 2). Even 55% of the experts had no idea about the term. Only one expert conveyed a partly application of Industry 4.0 ideas in the company in connection with an ERP system. Another interviewee justified the non-application with absent customer requirements. When customers demand and pay for the application of Industry 4.0 elements caused by the supply-chain, the service supplier of course would invest in appropriate IT support systems. But there is no intrinsic motivation for investing in any Industry 4.0 applications.

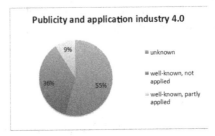

Fig. 2. Results expert interviews

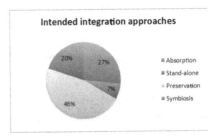

Fig. 3. Integration approaches of interviewees

Figure 3 shows the intended integration approaches in the experts´ companies. On first sight the low significance of Industry 4.0 might come along with stand-alone and preservation approach. But nearly half of the companies intend to integrate with absorption or symbiosis approach. This means these companies have to cope with process design, process harmonization and connected IT support systems anyway.

5 Discussion

Industry 4.0 is still a relevant topic. Although the numbers of publications seem to decrease in 2016 after a peak in 2015, the topic is of enormous interest. Many parts of Industry 4.0 infrastructure are already available in companies, but until the realization of the vision is still a long way [13]. Industry 4.0 is at an early stage of implementation in production industry, as well as in human environment and scientific research yet [39, 40]. The results of Fig. 1 compared with google trend analysis shows a similar result: the german term shows a stagnating interest in time response, whereas the English term demonstrates a still growing interest especially in Germany, Japan and USA [41].

However there seem to be a gap between scientific publications and Industry 4.0 knowledge in practice. 55% of the interviewed experts have no association about the term "Industry 4.0". Further 36% of the experts do not regard Industry 4.0 as relevant enough for investigating in their company. This confirms a survey of Fraunhofer-Institut für Arbeitswirtschaft und Organisation IOT in 2013 with the result, that 60% of respondents are not familiar with the term "cyber-physical system" [13].

The basic cause is supposed to the fact that all interviewees are derived from the service sector. Industry 4.0 has primarily been developed for production industry, so the service sector is one step behind. Downstream markets (activities after production) could use the opportunity to widen their portfolio with the development and offer of new services. Especially small and medium-sized services companies and start-ups could develop innovative services with the Big Data and intelligent devices in the B2B (Business-to-Business) area [6]. But to catch this chance, service companies have to design their processes and organization due to the new Industry 4.0 elements [5]. At the same time companies see in the process organization the introduction of software and simulation of processes as secondary compared with the increase of organizational effectiveness and continuous process management [42]. Hence the focus of service companies was concentrated on process-oriented organization and less on innovation.

Industry 4.0 might be accompanied with resistance of the employees. It is expected that the way people work is changing. The employee will set apart with mobile devices such as smartphones and tablets [43]. Thus, new communication technologies and communication species require both, an appropriate infrastructure and acceptance by the employees. However employees will stay irreplaceable, but their tasks will change [8]. The ideal situation is, however, the task design follows the "Best fit", and so the strengths and interests of employees and technology are used and best suited to each other. Therefore, technology, organization and qualification should always be developed hand in hand [44]. For acceptance, the process quality helps. A study shows that employees consider process quality and the associated tasks and fulfillment of customer orientation as very important by structural changes [45]. *"Surprises disturb the peace"* [46]. The employees should be involved and informed at an early stage in order to give them the chance of a certain preparation time of changes.

With the increasing globalization of production companies the requirements to service companies are increasing [47]. As a part of the integration process the merged company has the chance of a comprehensive modernization of outdated information systems and thus possibly the opportunity to catch up a competitive disadvantage [27]. The various information and communication tools (e.g. ERP systems) must be linked not only within the existing business processes, but possibly to external partners, too. In long-term consideration companies shall incorporate suppliers and customers automatically in relevant internal processes to share access to the same information [48]. Progressively less standardized, but much more knowledge-based services are required, with corresponding additional complexity, but also complicate the entry barriers in the market. With knowledge-intensive, low standardized activities can be higher profit margins and higher profitability achieved [47], which is just for European companies in the global context of interest.

After harmonizing the processes, the IT infrastructure should support the underlying processes to achieve the business objectives [49]. *"IT standardization follows process standardization – not vice-versa"* [50] – although both are different, there is a strong relationship. As the control and coordination of processes in smart factories take place in real-time, individual process steps have to be standardized first [48]. Process standardization is often facilitated by IT [51]. Not for nothing is IT identified as one of six core elements of Business Process Management [52]. The linkage of IT systems with BPM is already today one of the most advanced methodologies. Process modeling or process simulation with automated workflow systems is strongly oriented on the existing business processes and the company´s organization under the use of computer systems and its applications [53].

Returning to Quality 4.0, arising from Industry 4.0, huge opportunities in knowledge management and risk management could be achieved with a smart information technology [54]. Due to the existing Big Data risk management is greatly mathematized and professionalized so that a new dimension of risk assessment will be available. An own and increased focus for this topic is dedicated, conceivable is an expert with the interface Risk Management and Data Scientist [54]. Already today numerous metrics through PDM (Product data management), ERP and CAQ systems are offered to the management system that support both, productivity and efficiency in the identification of process and development defects and makes the quality system measurable and its strategic direction defined [55].

The results show far too low knowledge about Industry 4.0 in the companies. The integration of Industry 4.0 effectively did not take place in any of the respondents' organizations yet.

Especially quality managers shall be well informed about new trends and developments in quality management environment. "Industry 4.0" and ideally "Quality 4.0" should be well known buzz phrases for each single employee in a process or quality department and IT department, as well as organizational development or in the post-merger integration often involved external consultants. This group of people should be well informed and in a strong interchange to each other to sensibilize senior management about the importance and influence of Quality 4.0, either there is a decision against Quality 4.0 in a company at the moment.

6   Conclusion and Limitations

The objective of this article is to discover the significance of Industry 4.0 respectively Quality 4.0 in the service sector and its influence during process harmonization. A systematic literature review and empirical analysis were executed. As a central result can be concluded there is stagnation in publications of "Industry 4.0" articles since 2015 and quite few results for "Quality 4.0". However Industry 4.0 is at an early stage of implementation even in production industry, thus it is still of enormous interest.

Within practioners there seem to be a significant lack of understanding Industry 4.0. The majority of consulted experts did not have any association with the term "Industry 4.0". A massive elucidation and information about Industry 4.0 in practice is demanded. The key result of expert interviews demonstrates that Industry 4.0 has no influence in process harmonization, corresponding elements and supportive IT tools. In none of the service organizations are any intrinsic endeavors for implementing Industry 4.0 elements intended. Downstream markets could profit immense from the accompanied potential, e.g. with the implementation of corresponding ERP systems.

The author would like to indicate to following limitations: The number of experts is too low to conclude to a broad mass. On the other hand a survey of Fraunhofer IOT came to the same result. The second limitation lies in the literature review. A broader survey of more databases might reach a more detailed result. But the intended scope of the literature review is covered.

This article represents an important contribution to the significance of Industry 4.0 in practice of service companies in the post merger integration. Although the sum shows a publication decrease in 2016 there is still much room for further research. This study implies following suggestions: First, more investigation is needed to find out more about the interface of Industry 4.0 and process harmonization. Second, research should focus on the influence of Industry 4.0 in direction of quality management in the sense of Quality 4.0. Third, the readiness of service companies for Quality 4.0 aspects is not given at the moment, therefore corresponding methodologies and tools are required. The poor search results for "Quality 4.0" demonstrate a wide field of future research. Fourth, further research is needed how service companies can make themselves ready for the cyber-physical future.

References

1. Chang, S.-I., Chang, I.-C., Wang, T.: Information systems integration after merger and acquisition. Ind. Manag. Data Syst. **114**, 37–52 (2014)
2. Mendling, J., Komus, A., Gadatsch, A.: Ohne Menschen keine Transformation - Warum der Faktor Mensch weiterhin den Erfolg von BPM bestimmt. QZ Qual. und Zuverlässigkeit. **61**, 31–33 (2016)

3. Binner, H.F.: Industrie 4.0 bestimmt die Arbeitswelt der Zukunft. e i. Elektrotechnik und Informationstechnik. **131**, 230–236 (2014)

4. Pohland, S.: Flexibilisierung von Geschäftsprozessen Konzepte und Praxisbeispiele. Oldenbourg Wissenschaftsverlag, München (2009)

5. Schönreiter, I.: Bedarfe zur Prozessharmonisierung in fusionierten Dienstleistungsunternehmen im Zeitalter Quality 4.0. In: Winzer, P. (ed.) Herausforderungen der Digitalisierung, pp. 35–49. Shaker, Aachen (2016)

6. Kargermann, H., Wahlster, W., Helbig, J.: Umsetzungsempfehlungen für das Zukunftsprojekt Industrie 4.0. Forschungsunion, Berlin (2013)

7. BMBF: Industrie 4.0 Innovationen für die Produktion von morgen. Bundesministerium für Bildung und Forschung (BMBF), Bonn (2014)

8. Haddara, M., Elragal, A.: The readiness of ERP systems for the factory of the future. Procedia Comput. Sci. **64**, 721–728 (2015)

9. BMBF: Plattform Industrie 4.0. http://www.plattform-i40.de/I40/Navigation/DE/Industrie40/WasIndustrie40/was-ist-industrie-40.html

10. Koch, V., Kluge, S., Geissbauer, R., Schrauf, S.: Opportunities and challenges of the industrial internet (2015)

11. Sendler, U.: Industrie 4.0 Beherrschung der industriellen Komplexität mit SysLM. Springer Vieweg, Berlin [u.a.] (2013)

12. Bruhn, M.: Qualitätsmanagement für Dienstleistungen: Grundlagen, Konzepte, Methoden. Springer-Verlag, Berlin [u.a.] (2013)

13. Spath, D., Ganschar, O., Gerlach, S., Hämmerle, M., Krause, T., Schlund, S.: Produktionsarbeit der Zukunft - Industrie 4.0 (2013)

14. Menrath, M., Metzger, M., Meentken, F.: Globales Qualitätsmanagement in der Produktherstellung. In: Jochem, R., Menrath, M. (eds.) Globales Qualitätsmanagement: Basis für eine erfolgreiche internationale Unternehmensführung, pp. 275–356. Symposion, Düsseldorf (2015)

15. VDE: Industrie 4.0 kommt bis 2025 und stärkt die deutsche Wirtschaft. http://www.vde.com/de/Verband/Pressecenter/Pressemeldungen/Fach-und-Wirtschaftspresse/2015/Seiten/25-15.aspx

16. Glück, M.: Wie entwickelt sich eine Qualität 4.0? QZ Qual. und Zuverlässigkeit **60**, 39–43 (2015)

17. Artischewski, F.: Qualitätssicherung 4.0 – moderne Ansätze und Anforderungen der Qualitätssicherung im Kontext von Industrie 4.0. Fraunhofer-InstItut Für Fabrikbetr. und -automatIsIerung IFF, Magdebg. **8**, 25–30 (2015)

18. Bracke, S.: Qualitätsmethoden im Diskurs zwischen Wissenschaft und Praxis Bericht zur GQW-Jahrestagung 2015 in Wuppertal. Shaker, Aachen (2015)

19. Jochem, R., Knothe, T.: FAQ - Prozessmanagement: 100 Fragen - 100 Antworten. Symposion, Düsseldorf (2014)

20. Jochem, R., Geers, D.: Was versteht man unter Wirtschaftlichkeit von Qualität? In: Jochem, R. (ed.) Was kostet Qualität? Wirtschaftlichkeit von Qualität ermitteln, pp. 27–54. Hanser, München (2010)

21. Müller-Stewens, G.: Mergers & Acquisitions Analysen. Trends und Best Practices. Schäffer-Poeschel, Stuttgart (2010)

22. Haspeslagh, P.C., Jemison, D.B.: Managing acquisitions: creating value through corporate renewal. The Free Press, New York (1991)

23. Jansen, S.A.: Mergers & Acquisitions Unternehmensakquisitionen und -kooperationen; eine strategische, organisatorische und kapitalmarkttheoretische Einführung. Gabler, Wiesbaden (2008)

24. Marchand, M.: When the south takes over the north: Dynamics Of up-market integrations by emerging multinationals. M@n@gement. **18**, 31–53 (2015)
25. Marks, M.L., Mirvis, P.H., Brajkovich, L.F.: Making mergers and acquisitions work: strategic and psychological preparation [and Executive Commentary]. Acad. Manage. Exec. **15**, 80–94 (2001)
26. Vieru, D., Rivard, S.: The dilemma of integration versus autonomy: knowledge sharing in post-merger is development. In: Twenty Ninth International Conference on Information Systems, Paris, pp. 1–11 (2008)
27. Wirtz, B.W.: Mergers & Acquisitions Management. Springer Gabler, Wiesbaden (2014)
28. Webster, J., Watson, R.: Analysing the past to prepare for the future: writing a literature review (2002)
29. Cooper, H.M.: Organizing knowledge syntheses: a taxonomy of literature reviews. Knowl. Soc. **1**, 104–126 (1988)
30. Brocke, J., Simons, A., Niehaves, B., Niehaves, B., Reimer, K., Plattfaut, R., Cleven, A.: Reconstructing the giant: on the importance of rigour in documenting the literature search process (2009)
31. Mayring, P.: Qualitative Inhaltsanalyse: Grundlagen und TechnikenGrundlagen und Techniken. Beltz, Weinheim [u.a.] (2015)
32. Mayring, P.: Qualitative Content Analysis: Theoretical Foundation, Basic Procedures and Software Solution, Klagenfurt (2014). www.beltz.de
33. Friedrichs, J.: Methoden empirischer Sozialforschung. Westdt. Verl, Opladen (1990)
34. Borchardt, A., Göthlich, S.E.: Erkenntnisgewinnung durch Fallstudien. In: Albers, S., Klapper, D., Konradt, U., Walter, A., Wolf, J. (eds.) Methodik der empirischen Forschung, pp. 37–54. Dt. Univ.-Verl, Wiesbaden (2006)
35. Stier, W.: Empirische Forschungsmethoden. Springer, Berlin [u.a.] (1996)
36. Esser, H.: Differenzierung und Integration sozialer Systeme als Voraussetzungen der Umfrageforschung: Differentation and integration in social systems as prerequisites of survey research. Zeitschrift für Soziologie ZfS. **4**, 316–334 (1975)
37. Raab-Steiner, E., Benesch, M.: Der Fragebogen von der Forschungsidee zur SPSS-Auswertung. facultas.wuv, Wien (2012)
38. Weiss, H.: Industrie 4.0 - ein deutscher Begriff. http://www.vdi-nachrichten.com/Technik-Gesellschaft/Industrie-40-deutscher-Begriff
39. Roblek, V.: A complex view of industry 4.0. SAGE Open. **6**, 1–11 (2016)
40. Sauer, O.: Information technology for the factory of the future – state of the art and need for action. Procedia CIRP. **25**, 293–296 (2014)
41. Google Trend Analysis
42. Dombrowski, J., et al.: Prozessorganisation in deutschen Unternehmen - Eine Studie zum aktuellen Stand der Umsetzung. Zeitschrift Führung + Organisation (zfo), 84, pp. 63–69 (2015)
43. Lingitz, L., Hold, P., Glawar, R., Sihn, W.: Integration von Lösungskompetenz operativer Mitarbeiter des Shop-Floors in die Produktionsplanung und -steuerung. In: Industrie 4.0 Wie intelligente Vernetzung und kognitive Systeme unsere Arbeit verändern, pp. 177–197. Gito, Berlin (2014)
44. Müller, E., Riedel, R.: Humanzentrierte Entscheidungsunterstützung in intelligent vernetzten Produktionssystemen. In: Industrie 4.0 Wie intelligente Vernetzung und kognitive Systeme unsere Arbeit verändern, pp. 211–237. Gito, Berlin (2014)
45. Picot, A., Freudenberg, H., Gassner, W.: Management von Reorganisationen Maßschneidern als Konzept für den Wandel. Gabler, Wiesbaden (1999)
46. Juran, J.M.: Der neue Juran Qualität von Anfang an. Verl. Moderne Industrie, Landsberg/Lech (1993)

47. Jochem, R., Menrath, M.: Globales Qualitätsmanagement: Basis für eine erfolgreiche internationale Unternehmensführung. Symposion Publ., Düsseldorf (2015)
48. Reuther, S.: On the road to the Smart Factory. Brauwelt Int. 228–231 (2015)
49. Seidenschwarz, W.: Marktorientiertes Prozessmanagement wie Process Mass Customization Kundenorientierung und Prozessstandardisierung integriert. Vahlen, München (2008)
50. Ricken, A., Steinhorst, A.: Standardization or Harmonization? You need Both. BPTrends, pp. 1–5 (2005)
51. Beimborn, D., Joachim, N., Gleisner, F., Hackethal, A.: The role of process standardization in achieving IT business value. In: Proceedings of the 42nd Annual Hawaii International Conference System Science HICSS, pp. 1–10 (2009)
52. Rosemann, M., Brocke, J.: The six core elements of business process management. In: Brocke, J., Rosemann, M. (eds.) Handbook on Business Process Management 1. IHIS, pp. 105–122. Springer, Heidelberg (2015). doi:10.1007/978-3-642-45100-3_5
53. Aagesen, G., Krogstie, J.: BPMN 2.0 for modeling business processes. In: Brocke, J., Rosemann, M. (eds.) Handbook on Business Process Management 1. IHIS, pp. 219–250. Springer, Heidelberg (2015). doi:10.1007/978-3-642-45100-3_10
54. Vocelka, A.: Integriertes Risikomanagement im Zeitalter von Big Data. In: Horváth, P., Michel, U. (eds.) Controller Agenda 2017 Trends und Best Practices, pp. 59–75. Schäffer-Poeschel Verlag, Stuttgart (2014)
55. Meentken, F., Rinaldi, F., Jost, R.: Smart Quality verbindet weltweit. QZ Qual. und Zuverlässigkeit. **60**, 30–34 (2015)

Understanding the Flexibility of Cloud ERP Software

Dawid Nowak[✉] and Karl Kurbel

European University Viadrina Frankfurt (Oder), 15230 Frankfurt (Oder), Germany
{danowak,kurbel.bi}@europa-uni.de

Abstract. Enterprise resource planning (ERP) systems in the cloud are nowadays offered with different service models and deployment options. Depending on these models and options, the degree of flexibility varies as to what the customer gets with regard to customization requirements. Based on an empirical study of cloud ERP systems on the market, the paper focuses on the customization approaches applied by the vendors and the resulting degree of flexibility for adapting specific system elements. Our research shows that different customization options, beyond parameter-based configuration, are usually incorporated into the vendors' customization strategies. The flexibility depends to a large extent on the maturity of the system, i.e., is it a cloud-native or a cloud-enabled solution.

Keywords: Customization · Flexibility · ERP · Cloud · SaaS · On-demand

1 Introduction

In the past, enterprise resource planning (ERP) systems were usually installed as *on-premise* systems, i.e. on computers and infrastructure located on the customer's premises. More recently, alternative software delivery models have emerged, allowing software vendors to reach larger numbers of customers. Based on the cloud computing paradigm, business software is now also provided in the form of on-demand services via the Internet [1, p. 132]. In recent years, interest among software vendors in general and ERP vendors in particular to employ cloud-based delivery models for their products has risen [2]. More and more ERP systems are nowadays offered as "cloud" or "on-demand" solutions.

Various approaches exist as to how software can be deployed in the *cloud* and how it can be delivered to the customer (cf. [3]). A common distinction is based on the NIST's (National Institute of Standards and Technology) definition of service models: Software-as-a-Service (SaaS), Platform-as-a-Service (PaaS), and Infrastructure-as-a-Service (IaaS). These service models mainly use private, public, or hybrid clouds [4].

Regardless of how an ERP system is made available to the customer, it must be flexible in the sense that it allows adaptation to the specific requirements of the customer's organization. The process of adapting a business system to the needs of the client is usually called *customization* [5, p. 167]. Hence, the term *customizability* (or *flexibility* [1]) stands for a business system's internal property that it can be modified according to the customer's requirements.

© Springer International Publishing AG 2017
F. Piazolo et al. (Eds.): ERP Future 2016, LNBIP 285, pp. 135–146, 2017.
DOI: 10.1007/978-3-319-58801-8_12

To reach an appropriate level of flexibility, the customization approach must be planned early in the software life cycle and anchored in the architectural design of the software [6, p. 19]. However, few cloud ERP systems on the market were designed from scratch, in accordance with the SaaS delivery model. As can be seen from market analyses [2, 7], many former on-premise systems are nowadays also being offered as cloud solutions. Traditional ERP vendors increasingly modify their on-premise systems in order to realize the economies of scale of cloud computing.

According to the *maturity model* [8], an on-premise system can be transformed in steps to be fully compliant with the SaaS model. This transformation process often requires a significant reengineering of the system architecture. The highest maturity level is reached when the system is capable of serving multiple clients with only one software instance, ensuring high scalability and configurability.

However, many cloud-enabled systems are not capable of serving multiple clients with the same software instance or do not scale as effectively as fully compliant SaaS applications. In the sense of SaaS compliancy, their architecture is still immature, forcing the vendor to invest in further development to truly benefit from the advantages of SaaS [3].

Despite the fact that many authors acknowledge the need to customize cloud-based ERP systems, this problem has not been examined thoroughly. In particular, research investigating different customization approaches and/or existing cloud ERP systems with respect to the flexibility they provide is lacking (cf. [1, p. 139], [9, p. 4223]). This paper aims to fill the gap with the help of a survey-based study, focusing on cloud ERP systems that are available on the market.

The paper is organized as follows. In the next section, our preliminary research is presented, and common customization tasks and approaches are described. Section 3 outlines the design of our study and provides an overview of the data gathering process. In Sect. 4, the results of the study are statistically analyzed, and findings are discussed. Section 5 concludes the paper with a brief summary and an outlook to future research.

2   Background

2.1   Previous Research

Authors focusing on the adoption of cloud-based ERP systems usually name customization as one of the major challenges (e.g. [10, p. 154], [11, p. 433]). Some researchers (e.g. [2, 12, 13]) state that ERP systems provided as SaaS are not suitable for customers requiring extensive customization. Limited adaptability, problems to integrate them with other business software (cf. [14, p. 8]), and lack of customization features are mentioned as further drawbacks [1].

On the other hand, cloud ERP vendors claim that their systems offer comprehensive adaptability and flexibility (e.g. [15, 16]). While some studies (e.g. [10, 12]) conclude that customization beyond a few predefined configuration options is not provided, others show that customization techniques known from on-premise ERP systems can be applied [17].

In-depth studies focusing on the customizability of cloud-based ERP systems are rare. Exceptions are [18, 19], where innovative customization concepts and tools beyond the customization framework known from on-premise systems are presented.

In summary, previous research on the customizability of cloud-based ERP systems is inconclusive, indicating that further investigations are needed. It should also be noted that the continuing growth of the cloud market and the diversity of deployment options make it difficult to interpret other research. Authors often fall short of providing information about the underlying service-delivery and cloud-deployment models. Some studies regarding customization of cloud-based ERP systems are mostly based on one specific ERP system (cf. [20, 21]).

Customizability of cloud applications in general is a broadly discussed topic in academia. Most researchers exhibit skepticism, for the same arguments that are in place for the SaaS model.

Software-as-a-service has been the preferred way of providing an ERP system to the customer via the cloud, as this delivery model allows the vendor to exploit economies of scale well. Nowadays, many vendors extend their application software with PaaS services [9, p. 4222] or even IaaS [7]. With PaaS and IaaS, more powerful customization approaches can be incorporated into the vendor's customization strategy. On the customer's side, deployment in a private cloud [2, p. 13] is gaining popularity, making more individualization within the software possible.

Bearing this in mind, the question of how much flexibility cloud ERP systems do provide is not straightforward to answer.

2.2 Common Customization Requirements

The main reason for the need to customize are misalignments between the business requirements of the client and the standards contained in the ERP system. The typology provided by [22, p. 48] distinguishes misalignments related to the data layer, the logic layer, and the presentation layer.

According to Mijac et al. [1, p. 135], customization requirements regarding cloud-based ERP systems do not differ from the requirements regarding on-premise systems. In both cases, the vendor has to provide an adequate degree of flexibility to be able to ensure a satisfactory system adoption level [10, 23].

Taking into account the diversity of individual companies, it is not possible to address all potential customization requirements within this paper. Instead, our study focuses on common customization tasks that are typical for many ERP implementations.

Based on a literature study (namely [6, 24–26]), common customization requirements were identified. Next, these requirements were grouped into nine categories, according to the system element(s) they affect. Table 1 summarizes the categories.

Table 1. Common customization requirements

System element	Customization requirement
Analytics	Defining individual key figures, diagrams, and reports. Extending dashboards and predetermined data sources
System windows	Adapting the user interface according to the business requirements. This comprises adjustments to the corporate identity and nomenclature, repositioning or activation/deactivation of input fields, and more
Business processes	Adapting preconfigured workflows to reflect the business processes or procedures required by the organization
Custom functionality	Developing individual functional extensions and integrating these extensions with the system
Organizational structure	Adapting the organizational structure within the system to reflect the actual business organization
Business objects	Defining individual data structures and/or extension of standardized business objects with new data fields
Integration with other systems	Integrating the system with other business software and web-based services
Parameter settings	Configuring the system's look-and-feel through changing values of predefined system parameters
Set of system modules	Setting up an individual system from the set of predefined functional components (modules)

For each of the system elements in the first column of Table 1, the level of flexibility provided by the ERP systems under study will be described and discussed below (cf. Sect. 4.1).

2.3 Customization Approaches

Vendors of ERP standard software usually offer different customization approaches, based on their *customization strategy*. A customization strategy determines how and to which extent the system can be adjusted to the customer' needs (cf. [6, p. 19]). Studies of on-demand ERP systems usually differentiate only between *codeless* and *code-based* adjustments (e.g. [21]), stating that code-based adjustments are normally not feasible (e.g. [27]).

In earlier research on the customization of on-premise ERP systems, a number of typologies used by ERP vendors were identified (i.e. [28–31]). Some of these typologies, however, are not up-to-date any more, not suited for analyzing modern software [9, p. 4220]. Therefore, we use the reference model presented in [5], which appears to provide the most adequate categorization of customization options. Table 2 gives a brief overview of these options.

Table 2. Common customization approaches (based on [5])

Approach	Description
Composition	Putting together an individual set of predefined system components that together constitute a custom solution
Parametrization	Adjusting the system's functionality and data structures by setting values of predetermined system parameters
Model-based code generation	Automatic generation of program code and/or database schemata based on an information model. Adjustments are made on the level of the information model, which serves as input to code generation
Extension points	Extending the system's functionality through custom code embedded in predefined places of the ERP system's code (so called extension points, also known as user exits)
Application programming interfaces (APIs)	Developing code extensions that use pre-fabricated system components
Extension	Code-based development of new components outside the ERP system. New components provide functionality not available in the standard system
Code modification	Making changes directly in the ERP system's code

3 Study Overview

For the purpose of our study, a quantitative research approach based on a survey was applied. This approach seemed to be appropriate as the research strives to compare the customization strategies of many different vendors and to recognize overall patterns.

The initial step in preparing the study was to identify ERP vendors who make their offerings available in the cloud. This step was conducted based on an analysis of conference papers, journal articles, current market reports, ratings, etc. It ended with a sample of 33 vendors offering a portfolio of 37 cloud-based ERP systems.

In order to ensure high information quality, the study focused on persons with the necessary technical domain expertise, i.e. product managers, system architects, developers, and consultants. The respondents were chosen intentionally, based on a *purposive sampling* strategy [32, p. 231]. This strategy is most effective when the study comprises a domain where knowledgeable experts exists. For the purpose of the study, 98 practitioners on the vendors' side were identified and invited to participate in an online survey.

In addition to general questions regarding the system and service architecture, most survey questions were about particular customization options (cf. Sect. 2.2) and the customizability of individual system elements (cf. Sect. 2.3). The answers were measured on a five-point Likert scale (0 – "not supported" to 4 – "fully supported").

The survey returned 25 valid responses referring to 25 different cloud ERP systems. The gathered data were analyzed with the help of statistical software – IBM SPSS Statistics 23.

All ERP systems are cloud-based, however, their compliancy with the SaaS delivery model varies. 68% are *cloud-enabled*, which means that they were previously offered as on-premise systems. 32% are *cloud-native* solutions, i.e. designed for the cloud from scratch. While 48% of the systems are primarily offered in a public cloud, 52% are deployed in a (hosted) private cloud. According to the gathered data, 16% of the offerings are PaaS enabled.

4 Study Results

In this section, we present the results of the survey-based study and discuss the major findings.

4.1 Adaptation Possibilities

In the first part of the survey, questions referring to the flexibility of the systems were asked. Respondents had to rate the extent to which a particular system element can be customized by an *administrative user*. An administrative user is a user who has enough privileges and expertise to perform system changes affecting the entire company.

The survey results are shown in Fig. 1.

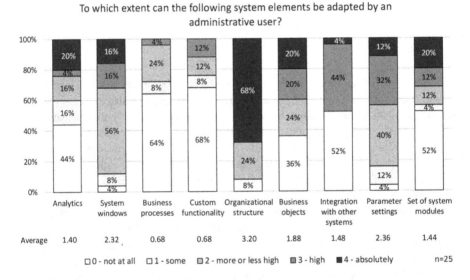

Fig. 1. Extent of client-side customizing

According to the respondents, administrators can perform changes to the system scope by modifying the set of system modules in 48%. Setting parameters is almost always available (96%). In nearly 96% of the cases, administrative users are allowed to adapt system windows, and in 92% to adjust the organizational structures.

64% of the systems allow the customer to individualize business objects. More than half (56%) let an administrative user perform changes to the way the analytics module works. Integration with other business software and web services is possible with nearly every other system (48%). Fairly limited are the options to include functional extensions (only 36%) and to adapt the workflows (32%) without the vendor's support.

With respect to the level of flexibility, the two highest-rated system elements are organizational structure (average 3.20) and parameter settings (2.36), followed by system windows (2.32) and business objects (1.88). Business processes were mostly perceived as providing little flexibility and hence rated low (0.68).

Splitting up the level of flexibility according to system layers, respondents rated flexibility of the user interface (2.34) higher than flexibility of the data layer (1.88) and flexibility of the business logic layer (1.55).

Comparing cloud-native with cloud-enabled ERP systems, statistically significant inhomogeneities in the mean ranks of set of system modules and integration with other business systems were identified.[1] For both of these system elements, cloud-native ERP systems exhibited significantly higher flexibility than cloud-enabled systems. This result suggests that vendors of mature cloud-based ERP systems do provide client-side administrators with appropriate tools.

This finding is supported by earlier research showing that some cloud-native ERP systems are equipped with built-in tools and features supporting individual arrangement of modules [21] and integration with other web-based services and applications [20]. Integrated tools not only reduce the complexity of customization, but also significantly speed up the customization and integration process.

Another finding worth mentioning is the important role of Platform-as-a-Service in client-side customizing. According to the study results, PaaS-based ERP systems provide administrative users with more comprehensive customization possibilities regarding almost all system elements under discussion.

Figure 2 illustrates the positive effect of a dedicated development platform around a cloud-based ERP system on the extent of adjustments an administrative user can make.

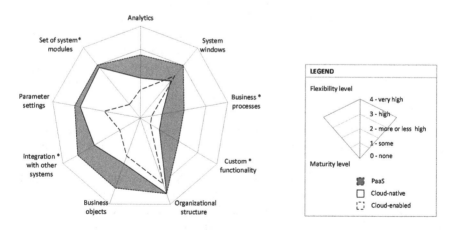

Fig. 2. Comparison of client-side customization depending on the maturity level

---

[1] Differences in mean ranks are statistically significant according to the Mann-Whitney U (MWU) test, p < 0.05.

The radar diagram compares the mean ranks calculated for three system groups – PaaS-based, cloud-native and cloud-enabled – and for each system element.

In an MWU test, statistically significant ($p < 0.05$) differences between PaaS and non-PaaS ERP systems in the extent of customization an administrative user can perform were detected. The test results indicate that PaaS-based systems allow more extensive functional changes, especially development of custom business and integration logic. In the diagram, those system elements for which PaaS-enabled ERP systems scored significantly higher than non-PaaS systems were marked with a * symbol.

4.2   Preferred Customization Approaches

The second part of the study compared general customization strategies followed by the vendors of cloud-based ERP systems.

When asked which customization approaches are incorporated in their strategy, most vendors named parametrization, composition, extension, and APIs (cf. Table 3).

Table 3. Customization approaches

Approach	Count	Percent
Composition	22	88
Parametrization	25	100
Model-based code generation	4	16
Extension points	10	40
APIs	20	80
Extension	21	84
Code modification	4	16

Surprisingly, 16% of the respondents named code modification as a viable customization option. These answers needed further clarification. We asked the respondents and were told that some modifications of the code are still possible when the system is deployed to a private cloud. This would actually require the vendor to offer code-based modifications as an additional service, beyond the standard subscription license. However, none of the vendors we asked allows their clients to make code changes on their own nor do they provide tools for code modification.

The survey results clearly confirm that various customization options, beyond parameter-based configuration, are in place. For each system in the study, at least three options were incorporated in the vendor's customization strategy and exposed to the customer.

Next, we tried to evaluate the importance of each customization option within the vendor's overall customization strategy. Figure 3 summarizes the results.

The highest-rated customization approaches were parametrization (3.28) and composition (2.96), followed by extensions (2.20) and application programming interfaces (1.76). Modification of the system's code (0.36) and model-based generation (0.20) received significantly lower values.

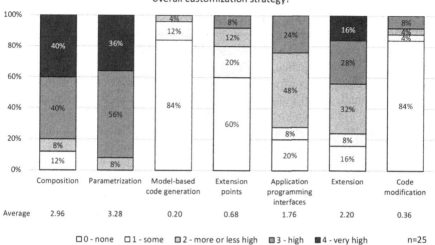

Fig. 3. Customization options

A general observation is that code-based customization was rated higher for private clouds than for public clouds, whereas the opposite is true for codeless customization. However, statistically significant (MWU test, p < 0.05) differences between private and public cloud deployment were only detected for parametrization and code modification.

These findings are in accordance with other research, [9, p. 4226], [21, p. 479], stating that vendors who offer their systems in public clouds mostly rely on parametrization as the preferred customization approach, refraining from code-based customization. Systems provided in public clouds are designed to support many clients with only one software instance (*multitenancy* concept [33]) and hence require a stable code basis, avoiding or minimizing customer-specific updates [34].

Comparing the results of the first and the second parts of our study, it can be concluded that vendors do realize that the degree to which they provide client-side customization features is an important factor for the client's willingness to adopt the system (cf. [10, 23]). This is indicated by the fact that those vendors who rated composition and parametrization higher also stressed that administrative users should be allowed to make more extensive changes regarding the set of system modules and the parameter settings (cf. Fig 2).

The test results show a high and significant (p < 0.05) correlation (Spearman's Rho, r = 0.680) between the role composition plays within the vendor's customization strategy and the extent to which the set of system modules can be changed by an administrative system user. In the case of parameter settings, a low but also significant correlation (Spearman's Rho, r = 0.359) between their role and the degree of flexibility provided to the customer was found.

5   Summary and Outlook

This paper discussed customization requirements and options offered by cloud-based ERP systems. Based on a survey, quantitative methods were used to analyze customization concepts of twenty-five cloud-based ERP systems.

Our discussion showed that, on the one hand, different customization options beyond parameter-based configuration are available for most cloud ERP systems. On the other hand, a gap between the customization strategies for mature and immature cloud systems can be observed. Especially differences regarding code-based and codeless customization approaches were identified. According to the study results, vendors who offer cloud-native ERP systems usually provide more extensive configuration and integration options than vendors whose solutions are cloud-enabled only.

Whereas many customization requirements can already be solved with the help of built-in customization tools, a development platform with services around the underlying ERP system allows the vendor to significantly extend the customization options offered to their customers.

In general, however, ERP systems available in the cloud differ significantly regarding the level of customization they allow. Our study showed that the fact whether an ERP system is deployed just as a service (SaaS) or with a platform around it (PaaS) has an influence on the degree of flexibility the customer gets.

Having this in mind, "cloud-based" ERP systems should not be seen as a unified architectural concept. In order to be able to adequately compare different cloud-based systems, these systems should be differentiated according to their maturity or the underlying cloud architecture.

Our study is exploratory and not exhaustive. The number of vendors and systems we were able to investigate in the different maturity categories are relatively small. The study should be seen as a first attempt to understand the differences in flexibility provided by cloud-based ERP systems and to explain possible reasons why academia and industry report about this quite differently (e.g. [1, 9, 11]).

In future research, we plan to extend the scope of the study to more vendors and cloud ERP systems, and to empirically evaluate the flexibility of different systems based on concrete case studies.

References

1. Mijač, M., Picek, R., Stapić, Z.: Cloud ERP system customization challenges. In: Central European Conference on Information and Intelligent Systems, Varazdin, Croatia, 18–20 September 2013 (2013)
2. Scavo, F., Newton, B., Longwell, M.: Choosing between cloud and hosted ERP, and why it matters. Comput. Econ. Rep. **34**(8), 1–15 (2012)
3. Jamshidi, P., Ahmad, A., Pahl, C.: Cloud migration research: a systematic review. IEEE Trans. Cloud Comput. **1**(2), 142–157 (2013)

4. Mell, P., Grance, T.: The NIST Definition of Cloud Computing. http://nvlpubs.nist.gov/nistpubs/Legacy/SP/nistspecialpublication800-145.pdf. Accessed 12 Aug 2016
5. Kurbel, K.E.: Enterprise Resource Planning and Supply Chain Management – Functions, Business Processes and Software for Manufacturing Companies. Springer, Heidelberg (2012)
6. Guo, C.J., Sun, W., Jiang, Z.B., Huang, Y., Gao, B., Wang, Z.H.: Study of software as a service support platform for small and medium businesses. In: Agrawal, D., Candan, K.S., Li, W.-S. (eds.) New Frontiers in Information and Software as Services: Service and Application Design Challenges in the Cloud. LNBIP, vol. 74, pp. 1–30. Springer, Berlin Heidelberg (2011)
7. Eggert, S., Schröder, E., Stritzel, M.: Besonderheiten von Cloud-ERP-Systemen. ERP Management 4(2013), 24–26 (2013)
8. Chong, F., Carraro, G.: Architecture Strategies for Catching the Long Tail. https://msdn.microsoft.com/en-us/library/aa479069.aspx. Accessed 12 Aug 2016
9. Uppström, E., Lonn, C.-M., Hoffsten M., Thorstrom, J.: New implications for customization of ERP systems. In: 48th Hawaii International Conference on System Sciences, pp. 4220–4229. IEEE, Washington (2015)
10. Lechesa, M., Seymour, L., Schuler, J.: ERP Software as Service (SaaS): factors affecting adoption in South Africa. In: Møller, C., Chaudhry, S. (eds.) CONFENIS 2011. LNBIP, vol. 105, pp. 152–167. Springer, Heidelberg (2012). doi:10.1007/978-3-642-28827-2_11
11. Saeed, I., Juell-Skielse, G., Uppström, E.: Cloud enterprise resource planning adoption: motives & barriers. In: Møller, C., Chaudhry, S. (eds.) Advances in Enterprise Information Systems II. Proceedings of the 5th International Conference on Research and Practical Issues of Enterprise Information Systems (CONFENIS 2011), pp. 429–434. CRC Press, Leiden (2012)
12. Schubert, P., Adisa, F.: Cloud Computing for Standard ERP Systems: Reference Framework and Research Agenda. Arbeitsberichte aus dem Fachbereich Informatik Nr. 16/2011. Institut für Wirtschafts- und Verwaltungsinformatik, Universität Koblenz-Landau (2011)
13. Peng, G.C., Gala, C.J.: Cloud ERP: a new dilemma to modern organisations? J. Comput. Inf. Syst. 54(4), 22–30 (2014)
14. Duan, J., Faker, P., Fesak, A., Stuart, T.: Benefits and drawbacks of cloud-based versus traditional ERP Systems. http://www.academia.edu/2777755/Benefits_and_Drawbacks_of_Cloud-Based_versus_Traditional_ERP_Systems. Accessed 12 Aug 2016
15. Hao, Y., Juell-Skielse, G., Uppström, E.: Cloud ERP development process model from the perspective of user organizations. In: Møller, C., Chaudhry, S. (eds.) Advances in Enterprise Information Systems II. Proceedings of the 5th International Conference on Research and Practical Issues of Enterprise Information Systems (CONFENIS 2011), pp. 407–428. CRC Press, Leiden (2012)
16. Asseco Solutions AG: ERP Akademie - Fit für APplus. https://www.applus-erp.de/download_file/force/345/. Accessed 12 Aug 2016
17. Iqbal, U., Uppström, E., Juell-Skielse, G.: Cloud ERP implementation challenges: a study based on ERP life cycle model. In: Møller, C., Chaudhry, S. (eds.) Advances in Enterprise Information Systems II. Proceedings of the 5th International Conference on Research and Practical Issues of Enterprise Information Systems (CONFENIS 2011), pp. 389–405. CRC Press, Leiden (2012)
18. Kurbel, K.E., Nowak, D.: Customization of on-demand ERP software using SAP business ByDesign as an example. In: Piazolo, F., Felderer, M. (eds.) Innovation and Future of Enterprise Information Systems: ERP Future 2012 Conference, Salzburg, Austria, November 2012, Revised Papers. LNISO, vol. 4, pp. 289–297. Springer, Berlin Heidelberg (2013)

19. Ortner, W., Krenn, G.: Are new configuration methods 'the key' to shorter ERP implementations? In: Piazolo, F., Felderer, M. (eds.) Multidimensional Views on Enterprise Information Systems. LNISO, vol. 12, pp. 23–40. Springer, Cham (2016). doi: 10.1007/978-3-319-27043-2_3
20. Elragal, A., Kommos, M.E.: In-House versus In-Cloud ERP systems: a comparative study. J. Enterp. Resour. Planning Stud. **2012**, 5–7 (2012)
21. Seethamraju, R.: Adoption of Software as a Service (SaaS) Enterprise Resource Planning (ERP) Systems in Small and Medium Sized Enterprises (SMEs). Inf. Syst. Front. **17**(3), 475–492 (2015)
22. Soh, C., Kien, S.S., Tay-Yap, J.: Enterprise Resource Planning: Cultural Fits and Misfits: Is ERP a Universal Solution? Commun. ACM **43**(4), 47–51 (2000)
23. Xin, M., Levina, N.: Software-as-a-Service model: elaborating client-side adoption factors. In: Proceedings of the 29th International Conference on Information Systems, Paris, France, 14–17 December (2008)
24. Sekatzek, E.P., Krcmar, H.: Measurement of the standard proximity of adapted standard business software. Bus. Inf. Syst. Eng. **1**(3), 234–244 (2009)
25. Scherrer-Rathje, M., Boyle, T.A.: End-user perspective on ERP flexibility. In: Proceedings of the 2008 Conference, Production and Operations Management Division. Administrative Sciences Association of Canada, vol. 29(7), pp. 83–98 (2008)
26. Keckeis, J., Dolezel, M., Felderer, M.: Towards a concept for enterprise systems landscape testing. In: Piazolo, F., Felderer, M. (eds.) Multidimensional Views on Enterprise Information Systems. LNISO, vol. 12, pp. 133–146. Springer, Cham (2016). doi: 10.1007/978-3-319-27043-2_11
27. Nitu: Configurability in SaaS (Software as a Service) Applications. In: Proceedings of the 2nd Annual Conference on India Software Engineering Conference, Pune, India, 23–26 February (2009)
28. Davenport, T.H.: Putting the enterprise into the enterprise system. Harvard Bus. Rev. **76**(4), 121–131 (1998)
29. Brehm, L., Heinzl, A., Markus, M.L.: Tailoring ERP systems: a spectrum of choices and their implications. In: Proceedings of the 34th Annual Hawaii International Conference on System Sciences, pp. 1–9. IEEE (2001)
30. Heines, M.N.: Understanding enterprise system customization: an exploration of implementation realities and the key influence factors. Inf. Syst. Manage. **28**(2), 182–198 (2009)
31. Rothenberger, M.A., Srite, M.: An investigation of customization in ERP system implementations. IEEE Trans. Eng. Manage. **56**(4), 663–676 (2009)
32. Johnson, B., Christensen, L.: Educational Research: Quantitative, Qualitative, and Mixed Approaches, 4th edn. Sage, London (2012)
33. Bezemer, C.-P., Zaidman, A.: Multi-Tenant SaaS applications: maintenance dream or nightmare?. In: Proceedings of the Joint ERCIM Workshop on Software Evolution (EVOL) and International Workshop on Principles of Software Evolution (IWPSE), pp. 88–92. ACM (2010)
34. Hofmann, P., Woods, D.: Cloud computing: the limits of public clouds for business applications. IEEE Internet Comput. **14**(6), 90–93 (2010)

Author Index

Printed in the United States
By Bookmasters